W0230019

# Boundaries, Priorities, and Finding Work-Life Balance

# HBR Work Smart Series

*Rise faster with quick reads,
real stories, and expert advice.*

It's not easy to navigate the world of work when you're exploring who you are and what you want in life. How do you translate your interests, skills, and education into building a career you love?

The **HBR Work Smart Series** features the topics that matter to you most in your early career, including being yourself at work, collaborating with (sometimes difficult) colleagues and bosses, managing your mental health, and weighing major job decisions. Each title includes chapter recaps and links to video, audio, and more. The HBR Work Smart books are your practical guides to stepping into your professional life and moving forward with confidence.

### Books in the series include:

*Authenticity, Identity, and Being Yourself at Work*

*Bosses, Coworkers, and Building Great Work Relationships*

*Boundaries, Priorities, and Finding Work-Life Balance*

*Experience, Opportunity, and Developing Your Career*

# WORK SMART

*Tips for Navigating Your Career*

# Boundaries, Priorities, and Finding Work-Life Balance

**HARVARD BUSINESS REVIEW PRESS**
Boston, Massachusetts

**HBR Press Quantity Sales Discounts**

Harvard Business Review Press titles are available at significant quantity discounts when purchased in bulk for client gifts, sales promotions, and premiums. Special editions, including books with corporate logos, customized covers, and letters from the company or CEO printed in the front matter, as well as excerpts of existing books, can also be created in large quantities for special needs.

For details and discount information for both print and ebook formats, contact booksales@harvardbusiness.org, tel. 800-988-0886, or www.hbr.org/bulksales.

Copyright 2024 Harvard Business School Publishing Corporation

All rights reserved

Printed in India by Replika Press Pvt. Ltd.

10 9 8 7 6 5 4 3

No part of this publication may be reproduced, stored in or introduced into a retrieval system, or transmitted, in any form, or by any means (electronic, mechanical, photocopying, recording, or otherwise), without the prior permission of the publisher. Requests for permission should be directed to permissions@harvardbusiness.org, or mailed to Permissions, Harvard Business School Publishing, 60 Harvard Way, Boston, Massachusetts 02163.

The web addresses referenced in this book were live and correct at the time of the book's publication but may be subject to change.

Library of Congress Cataloging-in-Publication Data

Names: Harvard Business Review Press, issuing body.
Title: Boundaries, priorities, and finding work-life balance /
    Harvard Business Review.
Description: Boston, Massachusetts : Harvard Business Review Press,
    [2024] | Series: HBR work smart series | Includes index. |
Identifiers: LCCN 2023048562 (print) | LCCN 2023048563 (ebook) |
    ISBN 9781647827083 (paperback) | ISBN 9781647827090 (epub)
Subjects: LCSH: Work-life balance. | Decision making. | Time management.
Classification: LCC HD4904.25 .B678 2024 (print) | LCC HD4904.25 (ebook) |
    DDC 306.3/61—dc23/eng/20231207
LC record available at https://lccn.loc.gov/2023048562
LC ebook record available at https://lccn.loc.gov/2023048563

ISBN: 978-1-64782-708-3
eISBN: 978-1-64782-709-0

MIX
Paper | Supporting
responsible forestry
FSC
www.fsc.org    FSC™ C016779

# CONTENTS

SECTION 3

# Beating Burnout

# INTRODUCTION

# Finding Balance

by Russell Glass, CEO at Headspace

Boundaries. Priorities. Balance. If you had thrown these three words out when I entered the workforce, I wouldn't have known what you were talking about. Since I was about 13 years old, I've been driven by the magic of entrepreneurialism and the ability to solve problems by building companies. And for the first six years of my career, I navigated the workforce and the world of startups without any thought about my boundaries, work-life balance, or overall mental health. I worked until after midnight, thought about work through fitful sleep, and woke early to do it all again. When my first startup, a promising company focused on mobile app development, started to fail as the dot-com bubble popped, I chased the false notion that working harder was the answer.

After that failure, I spent the next 18 months analyzing what went wrong. I realized that much of the issue was the lack of the right workplace culture and values as well as the unsustainable approach that I was taking to being a leader and thus modeling across the organization. I decided that my next company was going to be different—sure, we'd work hard—but we'd be guided by the right values and cultural tenets. This approach supported a work model that was both sustainable and successful, and I felt balanced for the six years that we grew that company through ups and downs and ultimately hypergrowth.

Flash forward to 2014. My wife and I welcomed our third child into the world. I had just sold the company to LinkedIn— an incredible and life-changing accomplishment for me and my team. By all measures, I had succeeded. Yet, as a new employee at a much larger company, I began to notice feelings of stress and anxiety at work. I wasn't sleeping well, and suddenly little things felt more irritating. A small comment in a meeting could trigger a physical response—a tightening in my chest, faster breathing, and tunnel vision. I'd get stuck in reactive mode, trying to solve a challenge as fast as possible, but later I'd look back and regret the decision I'd made. As I navigated and led a team within a company 20 times bigger than my startup, it seemed like my cup was empty. I needed to figure out how to get back to my best self, both at home and at work. I chose to begin a mindfulness and meditation practice—and it made a huge difference.

I share this because it's important to realize that feelings and experiences like mine aren't abnormal. They are incredibly common—a perspective shared by dozens of professionals throughout this book. Research shows us that nearly 90% of employees have felt moderate to extreme stress in the past 12 months (February 2022–February 2023).[1] As we look to the newest generation entering the workforce, the figures are more jarring. Nearly 40% of Gen Z workers reported extreme stress—or stress every day—over that same time period.

The good news is, we're making progress addressing the issues. As a society, we're talking more about mental health, priorities, and balance in every aspect of our lives, including at work. In the same study, 91% of CEOs and 89% of employees agree that their company sufficiently supports their mental health compared with 94% and 67%, respectively, the previous year. Collectively, we've reduced the stigma around severe mental illness, in addition to normalizing the conversation around self-care and mental well-being. Boundaries and burnout are now common terms both in and outside of the workplace. Companies are doubling down on education and resources around these topics in addition to investing in self-care resources and better mental health care options for their employees. And employees have come to expect this from their organizations. We still have a long way to go, but the progress is encouraging.

As described by professors Ioana Lupu and Mayra Ruiz-Castro in chapter 1 of this book, it often takes a major life event for professionals to step back and reflect on their mental health and well-being. In my case, it was a couple of dramatic career shifts and the birth of a child, but I wish I'd been aware of the importance of boundaries, priorities, and balance much earlier on.

This book provides a tremendous resource for anyone regardless of career stage, but particularly for those just starting out. The pages that follow are filled with advice from world-renowned clinicians, corporate leaders, researchers, and experts, many of whom have dedicated their careers to improving workplace culture. Their guidance ranges from easy-to-implement strategies to reflection-oriented questions to help unearth answers from within. This is a guide that you can turn back to time and time again to learn how to set better boundaries between work and life, prioritize mental and physical health, battle burnout, and tackle your to-do lists in sustainable yet productive ways.

To our future generation of leaders, you have a tremendous opportunity—and in my opinion, a responsibility—not only to develop these critical skills for yourselves, but for the future teams and organizations you'll lead. With the global mental health crisis showing no signs of slowing down, we must all commit to shaping the future of work for the better. Our health and livelihood depend on it.

# Finding the Balance

# 1

# Work-Life Balance Is a Cycle, Not an Achievement

by Ioana Lupu and Mayra Ruiz-Castro

Despite the resounding evidence that working long hours can be harmful to both employees and employers, many professionals still struggle to overcome their assumptions—and their deeply-ingrained habits—around work hours.[1] What does it take to free yourself from these unhealthy patterns and reach a more sustainable, rewarding work-life balance?

To explore this question, we conducted almost 200 in-depth interviews with 78 professionals from the London offices of a global law firm and an accounting firm.[2] The majority of the interviewees described their jobs as highly demanding, exhausting, and chaotic, and they seemed to take for granted that working long hours was necessary for their professional success. However, about 30% of the men and 50% of women in our sample appeared to consciously resist overwork, describing a variety of strategies they developed for maintaining a healthier work-life balance. While the details of every individual case differed, our study suggested a common mental process that consistently helped this group of professionals to change the way they worked—and lived—for the better.

At a high level, our research shows that achieving better balance between professional and personal priorities boils down to a combination of reflexivity—or questioning assumptions to increase self-awareness—and intentional role redefinition.[3] Importantly, our research suggests that this is not a one-time fix, but rather a cycle that we must engage in continuously as our circumstances and priorities evolve. This cycle is made up of five distinct steps:

## 1. Pause and denormalize

Take a step back and ask yourself: *What is currently causing me stress, unbalance, or dissatisfaction? How are these circumstances affecting how I perform and engage with my job? How are they impacting my personal life? What am I prioritizing? What am I sacrificing? What is getting lost?* Only after you take a mental pause and acknowledge these factors can you begin to tackle them.

For instance, after several years of intense focus on her career, Maya,* a senior associate at a law firm, described feeling like she'd hit rock bottom. It was only at this point that she was able to

---

*Names have been changed for privacy.

recognize the toll her overwork had been taking on her family—and on her own mental and physical health:

> I was working quite long hours . . . it was a horrible sort of period . . . I think for me, that was the key point. I thought, "I am not doing this anymore, this is ridiculous." So I think from then on, I have taken a real step back.

Similarly, legal partner Kate told us that following the birth of her son, she experienced a major mental shift. She recognized that while the idea of "[I] must work, must work, must work" had been "indoctrinated" into her, she was now aware of the "clash" between this idea and where she was now as a mother. This life-changing event was the impetus she needed to take a step back, become aware of the mismatch between her current situation and her personal priorities, and begin to denormalize her habit of working long hours.

Of course, the professionals we talked to all led very busy lives. Many of them admitted that they didn't normally have the time or the energy to stop and reflect, and even expressed gratitude for the reflection space that the interview process itself allowed them. But while it's often a major life event—such as the birth of a child, or the death of a loved one—that catalyzes these realizations, it's possible to take a pause and start rethinking your priorities at any time. And although some professionals may be fine with long work hours, taking the time to think through these questions and acknowledge the trade-offs you've made (whether intentional or not) is helpful for anyone looking to discover alternative ways of working and living.

## 2. Pay attention to your emotions

Once you've increased your awareness of your current situation, examine how that situation makes you feel. Ask yourself, *Do I feel energized, fulfilled, satisfied? Or do I feel angry, resentful, sad?* For example, one respondent described his realization that his current work-life balance (or lack thereof) was engendering some pretty negative emotions:

> You feel resentful and bitter that something that funda-mentally isn't that important to the essence of life is stripping valuable time and minutes away from you . . . it's accentuated even more when you see someone who has lost their life or someone who has been told here's how much time remains on your clock. (Tobias, audits director)

A rational understanding of the decisions and priorities driv-ing your life is important, but equally important is *emotional* reflexivity—that is, the capacity to recognize how a situation is making you feel. Awareness of your emotional state is essential for determining the changes you want to make in your work and in your life.

## 3. Reprioritize

Increasing your cognitive and emotional awareness gives you the tools you need to put things into perspective and determine how your priorities need to be adjusted. Ask yourself: *What am I will-ing to sacrifice, and for how long? If I have been prioritizing work*

*over family, for example, why do I feel that it is important to priori-*
*tize my life in this way? Is it really necessary? Is it really inevitable?*
*What regrets do I already have, and what will I regret if I continue*
*along my current path?*

Our priorities often shift faster than our day-to-day time allo-
cation habits. The interviewees that described a more positive
work-life balance intentionally reprioritized how they spent their
time in a way that lined up with their true priorities. One par-
ticipant described how he still saw himself as a professional, but
had redefined that professional role to be more inclusive of other
valued roles, such as that of parent:

> The more I really understand what's important in life—
> and it's not really work—it's, you know, understanding the
> relative importance of work. I still get a lot of satisfaction
> and stuff from work, but it used to be everything to me,
> and now it's less than half to me. (Dan, audits director)

## 4. Consider your alternatives

Before jumping into solutions, first reflect on the aspects of your
work and life that could be different to better align with your
priorities. Are there components of your job that you would like
to see changed? How much time would you like to spend with
your family, or on hobbies? As one respondent illustrated, improving your situation takes time and experimentation:

> And it has taken me probably up to now, like my son is
> now two [years old], to get to a point where it's evolved
> into "this is how it works" [working more balanced

hours], and it has taken that sort of length of time, probably longer than I wanted it to, but it's there now. (Michael, audits director)

## 5. Implement changes

Finally, once you've recognized your priorities and carefully considered the options that could help you improve, it's time to take action. That can mean a "public" change—something that explicitly shifts your colleagues' expectations, such as taking on a new role that's designed to be less time-demanding or allows for a compressed week—or a "private" change, in which you informally change your work patterns without necessarily attempting to change your colleagues' expectations.

In our research, we found that both public and private changes can be effective strategies, as long as they're implemented in a sustainable manner. For private changes, that might mean setting self-imposed boundaries (such as choosing not to work on evenings, weekends, or during holidays)—and sticking to that decision—or turning down demands typically associated with your role (such as new projects or travel requests) even when you feel pressure to take them on. For public changes, rather than simply telling your supervisor that you want more time off or more flexible hours, securing support from key mentors, partners, and coworkers—or even better, formally applying for a new internal position or a flexible working scheme—is likely to result in more lasting change.

. . .

Importantly, the five steps outlined above are not a one-time activity, but rather a cycle of continuous reevaluation and improvement. Especially if you're under the influence of an overpowering culture of long work hours, it's easy to slide back into "business as usual" (whether that's a conscious or unconscious decision). In our interviews, we found that for people to make real changes in their lives, they must continuously remember to pause, connect with their emotions, rethink their priorities, evaluate alternatives, and implement changes—throughout their personal and professional lives.

## QUICK RECAP

Research shows that overwork isn't good for employees or their companies. Yet in practice, it can be hard to overcome unhealthy work habits and reach a more sustainable work-life balance. To achieve lasting change, view this process as a five-step cycle.

- Pause and denormalize to rethink your priorities at any time.

- Pay attention to your emotions to determine the changes you want to make in your work and in your life.

- Reprioritize how you spend your time in a way that aligns with your true priorities.

- Consider the alternatives before jumping into solutions.

- Implement changes publicly and privately. This might include imposing boundaries, turning down demands, securing support from mentors, or applying for a new internal position.

---

Adapted from content posted on hbr.org,
January 29, 2021 (product #H065F3).

Read more from Ioana Lupu on the habits that will help you create a good work-life balance and avoid burnout:

# 2

# Don't Feel Guilty for Prioritizing Yourself over Work

by Donna McGeorge

When you're young and just entering the workforce, it's natural to feel anticipation, eagerness, and even anxiety. You're likely to place specific expectations on yourself about what you want to achieve and how you want to grow. It's very easy to believe that hard work and long hours are what you need to do to get noticed and succeed.

But here's the thing: That's not true. Prioritizing your work over your physical, mental, and emotional self is a recipe for burnout, regardless of where you are in your career. The more you fall into the spiral of working long hours at the cost of your health, the harder it will become to recover from the long-term effects of overwork.

# Why Do We Feel Guilty About Prioritizing Life over Work?

As a society, many of us still equate the hours we work to our level of productivity. More generally, we equate "doing things" to being productive. How often have you reprimanded yourself for "wasting a weekend" because you spent it resting instead of making plans? It's this false notion of busyness that makes us feel ashamed for choosing respite over action. A quick look at the history of work can explain why.

During the Industrial Revolution, the average employee was expected to work close to 14 hours a day, six to seven days a week. It wasn't until the early 1900s that Henry Ford, the founder of Ford Motor Company, implemented the first 40-hour workweek. His decision wasn't benevolent. He believed he could sell more cars to his employees if they had more time off.

The idea of "hustle culture" became popular in the Great Recession of 2008.[1] The global economic crash pushed people to take on multiple jobs to survive. High unemployment rates and tough monetary conditions promoted overwork as a badge of honor that ultimately leads to success.

It took a global pandemic for companies and workers to shift this mentality. Today, employers have embraced remote or hybrid models of work and are beginning to recognize engagement and motivation as the key to employee well-being. There's even been talk about flexibility and trust as the main ingredients to productivity.

The point is: Our definition of "productivity" has evolved. In the last two years, companies have begun to emphasize making more impact over working more hours. You can choose to stay on that path. History has shown us, during hard economic times, we are pressured to shift back into a dangerous mindset, one that prioritizes work over well-being. But that doesn't need to be the case.

Your worth, talent, or value as an employee can be defined by the value your output creates, not how long it takes you to create it. But to do your best work—your most impactful work— you need to build a sustainable work-life balance that prioritizes you, your health, and your happiness.

## How Can You Prioritize Yourself?

Despite the demands of an ever-changing world, one thing is clear: Taking care of your health, regardless of what the culture tells you, is critical to your growth and success. You don't have to prove yourself before prioritizing yourself. In fact, the opposite is true: You need to prioritize yourself to perform at your best. The earlier you start to build healthy habits, the happier and more fulfilled you will be.[2]

While this work is not easy, taking small, deliberate steps is key to building a holistic, sustainable, and empowering identity. Here are four things you can do to make time for yourself without hampering your professional growth.

### 1. Build in time to do nothing

No, really. Nothing. Can you think back to a time when you just sat on the sofa, daydreaming, without the TV on or your phone nearby? How did that feel? With so many things vying for our attention, it's hard to get a few moments to ourselves. But cultivating this skill will teach you how to stay in the moment without dwelling on the past or worrying about the future. Sometimes, sitting with your thoughts can feel overwhelming, but there are ways to manage the hard feelings that arise.

One way to build a moment of genuine disconnect is to write things down as you think or feel them. Use a journal or a diary to honestly, and without much effort, scribble or doodle whatever crosses your mind or shows up in your body. Think of this as a daily "brain dump." It can help you literally wipe things off your mind and release the pressure to dwell, ruminate, or catastrophize.

For instance, if you're worried about a client meeting tomorrow, write about it. Putting your thoughts or fears on paper can take away their power and make them easier to acknowledge and manage. Words on a page are far less ominous than dark clouds floating in your mind.

Try to start or end your day with this practice.

> **PRO TIP:** You can also use this practice to record things that require your attention, that need organizing, or that you want immediate access to: client meetings, shopping lists, a big idea that randomly came to you, a business strategy, a new habit you're trying to build, or even a quote you like.

## 2. Learn to say no

When you're starting out in the workforce, everything feels important. A new project. A meeting. A stretch task. Each new opportunity may be your gateway to establishing your credibility and proving yourself at work. Often, this pressure makes us want to say yes more than we say no.

While that feeling is normal, and a healthy flow of work will keep you motivated and engaged, you need to understand your limits. To get better at declining requests without feeling guilty, reframe saying no as setting boundaries. To set healthy boundaries, you need to determine your physical and emotional bandwidth for doing things. Ask yourself:

- Who am I willing (or not willing) to give time to?

- What do I want (or not want) to do or achieve?

- When do I need to protect time, and when do I want to make myself available?

- Why would I give one person or activity my attention over another?

- What tasks or activities will (or will not) help me reach the outcomes I want?

Answering these questions will help you understand what energizes you, what drains you, and, ultimately, where you'd like to focus your time. Becoming aware of your own interests and disinclinations, and what tasks will help you reach your goals, is a part of the process. You need to acknowledge your limitations and be honest about them with yourself and others. This practice will make you a better team member, colleague, friend, and partner. It will give you the confidence to politely turn down requests.

▶ **PRO TIP:** When a senior colleague makes a request, we assume that we have no choice but to say yes. Instead, assume that they're a reasonable person who is willing to have a conversation with you about your priorities and reach a compromise. If you need to tell someone no, just explain why. Offer an alternative and ask them if the work can be done at a later time or, if the work is urgent, clarify that you can adjust your priorities based on team and business needs.

Sample language: "Thank you for thinking of me. Unfortunately, I don't have the bandwidth to take on an additional assignment this week, but if this task is an urgent one, I'm happy to discuss the timeline of my other projects and see how we can accommodate it."

## 3. Keep your work and life separate. Literally.

This is a hard one, especially if you're working in a hybrid or remote environment. The side effect of working from home has been that our spaces of sanctuary and relaxation now double as our offices, making it harder to draw clear physical boundaries between our different identities.

The solution? Become intentional about how you use different spaces within your home. When we work from the same space every day, our brain forms an association and develops specific cues that allow us to focus and become more productive.[3] The consistency makes it easier for us to separate our work from the rest of our home. If it's a shared space, like a dining room or kitchen table, put all your work gear away at the end of the day. Turning off your laptop and packing up your work notes will allow your brain to switch off more easily. Similarly, you can carve out a space where you never work—like your bed or couch.

➤ **PRO TIP:** Once you're done with work, try to turn off alerts or notifications on your phone. Even if you like scrolling through social media, learn to mute your emails, Slack, or other work applications to help you actually disconnect.

## 4. Understand what work really means to you

What do you want out of your career? While this may seem like a daunting question, gaining clarity around what you want right now and in the long term is necessary to build the right habits—habits that will help you reach that goal. The answer might not be obvious when you're just starting out, but as a first step, ask yourself a few questions:

- How do I want to be remembered in my work life? What legacy do I want to create?

- What about my job (outside of the actual work) energizes me?

- What work would I do if I knew there were no restrictions?

- Outside of work, what do I enjoy? Does my job allow me time to do those things?

- How would I spend my days if I didn't have to work?

Through this self-reflection, you may gain a better understanding of your long-term career vision, as well as discover and explore passions and interests outside of your job. The more time you spend in introspection about what a career means to you, the more you'll realize that your work life is merely a part of your identity—not the entirety of it. This will help you get crystal clear about what the best use of your time is and what stops you from wasting time on things, people, or activities that don't move you in the right direction.

> ➤ **PRO TIP:** This is not a one-time exercise. Your career vision will likely change over time, at different stages in your life, and that's okay. Try to reevaluate your values and goals a couple of times in a year. As you grow, consider setting specific goals around what you want from a job or an employer. This could look like a healthy work culture, better work-life balance, supportive colleagues, an inspiring boss or mentor, better compensation, or more equitable pay packages.

. . .

Know that there is no "right time" to look after yourself. The earlier you learn to prioritize your health and well-being, the better you will begin to feel about your work and your professional identity.

## QUICK RECAP

When we're starting out in the work world, we often equate the hours we spend at work to our productivity. But that's simply untrue. Not taking care of yourself early on can be a recipe for burnout. Here are four ways to prioritize yourself in a way that doesn't hurt your career growth:

- Disconnect from work by doing nothing. Think of this as a daily "wipe the mind" or "brain dump" to release the pressure to dwell on thoughts or feelings.

- Learn to say no and define your boundaries.

- Become more intentional about the physical spaces at home and how you wish to use them.

- Understand what your career goals and vision are and how they fit into the larger context of your life.

---

Adapted from content posted on hbr.org,
November 14, 2022 (product #H07CUZ).

**3**

# Balancing a Full-Time Job with School or a Side Hustle

by Elizabeth Grace Saunders

If you were part of the pandemic-era entrepreneurial boom, you may have taken up some work outside of your regular day job. Maybe you launched a side hustle with the goal of becoming your own boss. Maybe you decided to go back to school and pursue a part-time degree. You're not alone. Small business applications jumped 53% from 2019 to 2021; and graduate degree enrollment increased by 4.3% after years of descending.[1]

Even so, the initial luster of starting a venture outside of your nine-to-five is likely wearing off. The joyful string of "Congrats!" that sprang from your peers may be dampened by the reality of the grind: staying up late to complete assignments; the strain of balancing work, family, and friends; the to-do list that never seems to end.

Adding a major commitment to your life is never easy. Without the right tools, it can leave you feeling like you have no margin of error, or worse, that you're failing in everything.

As a time-management coach, I guide people facing this problem—people who are looking to find balance in their lives while going above and beyond in their pursuits. Getting a degree or starting a small business, especially while you're working full-time, poses unique challenges. That doesn't mean it's not possible. Here's what I find works.

## Acknowledge the challenge

Whether you're putting more time into your side hustle or working on a degree part-time, it's going to be a challenge to manage your time while also working a nine-to-five job. That's the reality, and you'll go further if you accept it rather than beating yourself up.

Most people working a full-time job have a few discretionary hours in the mornings and evenings. Depending on your personal commitments, you may also have another two to four hours to yourself on the weekend. That's not a whole lot of extra time when you factor in personal to-do items and family responsibilities.

If you feel like it's hard to keep up, that's because it is—and if you didn't have things on the side, you would have more freedom to engage in all sorts of activities. Acknowledge that this is your reality before you can take ownership of and maximize the time you *do* have available.

## Sharply define your work time

When you're excited about something big outside of your day job, it's tempting to do whatever you think is most important at any given time. But this method doesn't work well for most people. More often, it leads to analysis paralysis.

Many of my clients who tried this approach spent more time thinking about whether they should work on a report for their boss, post on their grad school forum, or attend a friend's birthday party than they did getting anything done. Others spent too much time on the activities they found most interesting (like searching LinkedIn for new business leads) and too little time on mundane but necessary activities (like answering the emails in their inbox or filing taxes).

When juggling multiple priorities, it's more powerful to sharply define when you're "on" and when you're "off." Create strict boundaries around the time you focus on your day job and the time you're free to devote to each of your personal priorities.

It's helpful to clarify the measures of success in your day job: important deadlines, annual goals, and any other touch points that matter to your boss. Emphasize the tasks that contribute to those things, and minimize as many volunteer commitments, special projects, or extra meetings as you can. When you have a side hustle or school to worry about, putting in extra hours at work isn't sustainable. You need to put those hours toward your other goals if you want to succeed without sacrificing your mental and physical well-being.

## Establish personal touch points

When you work a full-time job and have a large commitment on the side, you won't have the ability to participate in every family activity or social event, but you don't need to cut yourself off from society altogether.

What I find works best, in terms of a sustainable approach, is to first figure out what you need in order to take care of yourself:

- How many hours of sleep do you need a night?

- How much physical activity do you need?

- How present do you need to be with family and friends?

- What personal commitments are most important to you and your loved ones?

If you have a close circle of friends or people outside your immediate family, carve out a time to call them each week or designate a Friday Friend Happy Hour, where you make them a priority instead of allowing yourself to lose track of relationships.

Your commitments may vary depending on what you need to thrive. Once you determine what's most important to you, put it in your calendar as a recurring event and try to stick with it. You may not hit the mark every time, but if you're consistently and intentionally investing in your health and your most important relationships, you can sustain your physical and relational well-being even in this intense time.

## Dedicate time for school or your side hustle

Finally, just as you clearly defined time for your day job or personal touch points, I want you to dedicate time for school or your side hustle. Exactly what time you devote will depend on your preferences and constraints, but here are some common times that I've found work well for clients:

- Mornings before logging into work

- Evenings during the week

- One or two blocks of time on the weekends

- Lunch hours for more-discrete activities like posting on your class forum or returning client calls

Put these times in your calendar as meetings with yourself to devote to school or your business. Then stick to those hours and see if all you need to get done fits in that time. If it does, great! If not, then you'll need to consider finding additional hours for your special projects. Or you may need to reduce your expectations on certain things, like skimming a book instead of reading the whole thing, or extending the timeline for when you launch your new business.

This clarity helps you to decide specifically when you're working on your side projects instead of feeling like you're too tired or too busy with something else and then putting them off. Finally, it gives you the ability, if helpful, to physically separate yourself from home and go to a library, coffee shop, or coworking space to get your business or schoolwork done.

. . .

Balancing the demands of school or a small business on top of a full-time job and personal life is a lot. But with the right strategies, it is possible. Get clear on when you're working your day job, investing in life outside of work, and completing your side projects. Then let that structure support you through this fulfilling yet busy time.

## QUICK RECAP

Getting a degree or starting a small business, especially while you're working full-time, poses unique challenges. That doesn't mean it's not possible. Implement strategies to better manage your time while protecting your physical and mental well-being.

- **Accept the challenge.** Whether you're putting more time into your side hustle or working on a degree, it's going to be difficult to manage your time while also working.

- **Sharply define your work time.** Clarify the measures of success in your day job and emphasize the tasks that contribute to them.

- **Establish personal touch points.** Once you determine what's most important to you, put it in your calendar as a recurring event and try to stick with it.

- **Dedicate time to your side hustle or school.** This will vary depending on your schedule. Put these times in your calendar as meetings with yourself.

---

Adapted from content posted on hbr.org,
November 8, 2022 (product #H07C56).

# SECTION 2

# Set Better Boundaries

# 4

# A Guide to Setting Better Boundaries

by Joe Sanok

Like exercise, meditation, or budgeting, most of us know that having boundaries around our work and home lives is something we should probably do. Even so, finding the time to change unhealthy behaviors, learn, and build new habits is easier said than done.

In a world as fast-paced as ours, it's tempting to continuously look for the next shortcut or productivity tool to keep pace with the competition—but these "hacks" don't usually work. Pre-pandemic research indicated that many Americans were already sleeping less than previous generations, often to get extra work done.[1] Yet we were somehow increasingly unproductive. More-recent studies show that post-pandemic stress, anxiety, and insomnia have gone up.[2] Unsurprisingly, we are also more worried, caffeinated, and miserable. Our free time and physical activity have, on the whole, declined.[3]

A solution—boundaries—sits right in front of us. When we define what we need to feel secure and healthy, when we need it, and create tools to protect those parts of ourselves, we can do wonders for our well-being at work and at home—which, in turn, allows us to bring our best selves to both places. A boundary could be how we want our partners and peers to communicate with us, when we want our bosses to contact us, or even the days we most prefer to work versus rest.

So why do we have such a hard time setting boundaries?

In my experience counseling clients, business owners, and teams, I've learned that the practice of defining healthy boundaries can be triggering. Though boundaries represent different things to different people, they universally force us to examine toxic behaviors with roots in our past and can surface negative internal dialogues that are painful to address. For instance, a person who tends to be a people pleaser—an insecurity they likely developed in childhood—might have a hard time setting boundaries because they feel the need to continuously "give" to be worthy of others. Highly driven people, on the other hand, may see a boundary as a personal failure or an attack on their ego.

The good news is, no matter what skeletons hide in your closet, I have seen that even the most ingrained behaviors can be unlearned through setting boundaries. Here is what to do—and what not to do—as you get started.

## What Not to Do

At their core, boundaries are all about who we give power to. They force us to analyze why we may not be giving ourselves permission to work and live in the way that we feel is best for our well-being. If we're not deciding our lives, schedules, and workloads, who is? Boundaries allow us to decide when, how, and if we give this power away.

This is why, when setting boundaries, we typically go wrong when we expect other people to give us what we need as opposed to taking the initiative ourselves. We may ask our partners and peers to communicate with compassion, our bosses to send their last email no later than 5 p.m., or our workplaces for more flexible schedules—and still not see the outcomes we want.

In time, we get tired of asking. A boundary becomes another conversation we don't have the energy to see through. We give up or decide to just go with the flow and succumb to schedules, practices, or people who don't serve us. But this only leads to growing resentment.

## What to Do

One way to overcome these obstacles, and re-empower yourself, is to change your mindset around how boundaries work. Understand that boundaries are limits you identify for yourself and apply through action or communication. This doesn't mean you get everything you want when you want it. It means there are small things within your control that you can do to protect your time and energy.

To start, take a step back and begin by labeling your boundaries as "hard" or "soft."

- *Hard boundaries (nonnegotiables):* Boundaries that you are unwilling to compromise on and need to act on immediately. Think of them as things you will never do or never accept as reasonable. For example, I will never take on a consulting client who can meet me only on Fridays.

- *Soft boundaries (aspirations):* Boundaries that are more like wishes and that you are willing to compromise on. Think of them as goals you want to reach but are flexible around. For example, maybe you want to start leaving the office at 4:30 p.m. instead of 5:30 p.m., but other people (aka your manager) are involved in making that a reality. You can decide to take it slow and think about how you will initiate that conversation.

When you start to define boundaries as hard and soft, it will become easier to figure out your nonnegotiables versus your aspirations. This will allow you to confidently make choices that are aligned with your deepest needs and manage your energy as you work toward the rest.

Here's how to begin.

## Determine your top priorities in work and in life

What are the one or two things you are trying to get out of your personal life and your professional life? It could be as straightforward as spending more time with your family or finding a job that prioritizes your well-being. Naming what you can't live without, versus what you wish for, will help you distinguish the hard and soft boundaries you need to set.

To start, try a visualization exercise that I use with some of my clients. Imagine that your life as it is right now is no longer possible. Say you get laid off, you can't live in the town you live in, your partner breaks up with you, or you're forced to change careers. What would you do next? What would you miss? What would you not miss? What would feel the most exciting? What would feel the saddest?

Maybe you would choose a job closer to loved ones. Maybe you would miss having a compassionate boss but not miss constantly working overtime. Maybe you would finally feel free to explore other places, industries, and people. Now ask yourself: Out of all the things you listed, which reality can't you live without? Out of all the things you don't miss, which are you unwilling to go back to?

Your answers will reveal your high-level priorities as well as some lower-level aspirations that may be hidden below the safety net of your current situation.

## Test out one hard boundary

Now that you have a better idea of what your high-level priorities are, you can use what I call a "cutback experiment" to set hard boundaries to protect them. This exercise involves limiting tasks, interactions, or activities that are not the best use of your time. Being more selective about what and who you give your energy to will allow you to focus only on the items that give you the greatest return on your investment—whether that is greater achievement at work, more happiness at home, or some other reward.

For instance, let's say that your high-level priority is to protect the amount of energy you exert at work so that you are less drained upon arriving home. Think about everything you do at the office. Your tasks may feel equally important, but emails, heads-down work, and meetings can all have very different outcomes on your business's bottom line. You may set a hard boundary by saying no to meetings that you know are useless and replacing them with blocks of rest time on your calendar, or by putting an OOO message up after 5 p.m.

In your personal life, you may equally consider the relationships or activities that constantly drain you and drop them in lieu of spending time with the people who bring you joy. Essentially, you want to use hard boundaries to do less and conserve your energy while getting more important things done—that is, things that actually benefit you and your needs.

When I conduct this exercise with clients, this is where I often get pushback. People say, "Isn't it selfish to just focus on what I want?" My advice is for them to answer their own question—to think of this exercise as an experiment and gather the data.

After setting these boundaries, ask, "Did I feel more or less productive at work? Am I more or less refreshed in my role as a partner, a friend, or a parent?" You can always return to your old ways, but people frequently discover tasks or mindsets that no longer serve them.

## Practice a few soft boundaries

Next, think about your aspirations—the things you would like to change but don't need to change urgently. Maybe you want to get a better night's sleep, limit the amount of time you spend on social media, or spend fewer office hours answering tedious

emails. Are there soft boundaries you can set to feel more productive, creative, and rested at work and at home? Test them out.

For example, you could try not drinking caffeine after lunch
to improve your sleep, limit your social media scrolling to your
lunch break, or block an hour on your calendar to answer emails
in one go and stop as soon as that time is up.

Remember that at this stage, there is some flexibility with both
hard and soft boundaries. Test the waters to see how you feel and
how the results play out.

## Commit

You've now had some time to test out a few ways to protect your
time, energy, and well-being. Ask yourself: What did you learn?
What are a couple of boundaries, that if you set them, would
result in strong returns?

Commit to those for at least one quarter and see how you feel,
focusing on both the head and the heart, the qualitative and
quantitative. You can use the questions below to keep track of
your experience:

- What positive outcomes have come out of a boundary
  I set?

- What negative outcomes resulted from a boundary?

- How do I feel now versus at the beginning of this
  boundary experiment?

- What do I need to change or adjust to stay on track and
  address the negative?

- What boundaries do I want to stick to (hard boundaries) and which are more aspirational (soft boundaries)?

. . .

As you experiment with hard and soft boundaries, remember that the process is fluid. The focus is to gain a deeper understanding of what you actually want rather than what is handed to you by a boss, customer, partner, kid, friend, or society at large. When you step back, reflect, and evaluate your desires, you may discover that boundaries don't limit you. They give you the space to create the life you want to live.

## QUICK RECAP

Boundaries are limits we identify for ourselves and apply through action or communication. When we define what we need to feel secure and healthy when we need it, and create tools to protect those parts of ourselves, we can do wonders for our well-being at work and at home.

- Hard boundaries are your nonnegotiables. Soft boundaries are goals that you want to reach but are flexible around. Knowing the difference will allow you to make choices that are aligned with your needs.

- Practice setting one hard boundary to protect your high-level priorities by limiting interactions or activities that are not the best use of your time.

- Think about your aspirations. Are there soft boundaries you can set to feel more productive, creative, and rested at work and at home? Test them out.

- Pay attention to how these behavioral changes make you feel. Remember that the process is fluid and may change over time.

---

Adapted from content posted on hbr.org,
April 14, 2022 (product #H06ZNZ).

Listen to this episode from our *New Here* podcast to learn how
to better recognize and protect your boundaries at work:

# 5

# When Your Career Becomes Your Whole Identity

by Janna Koretz

Dan,* a partner at a Boston law firm, was due at the office, but instead, he was curled on his bathroom floor, unshaven and in his pajamas, crying into a towel.

It began slowly. In a meeting with a particularly pushy client, a thought bubbled up in his mind: "Why the hell am I even here?" From that moment, he noticed that his impatience, unhappiness, and frustration with his job grew deeper until all at once, he realized that he didn't find happiness or fulfillment in his work—and maybe he never had.

For someone who had built his entire idea of himself around his career, this thought sent Dan into an existential crisis. Who was he, if not a high-powered lawyer? Had he wasted so many

*Name changed to protect identity.

years working for nothing? Would he have had more friends and a happier family if he hadn't spent all those nights at the office?

Dan's story is not uncommon. Many people find themselves unhappy with their careers, despite working hard to get to their current position. Hating your job is one thing—but what happens if you identify so closely with your work that hating your job means hating yourself?

Psychologists use the term *enmeshment* to describe a situation where the boundaries between people become blurred and individual identities lose importance. Enmeshment prevents the development of a stable, independent sense of self. Dan had become enmeshed not with another person, but with his career.

As a psychologist, I specialize in mental health challenges associated with careers. People like Dan show up in my office every day. A particular confluence of achievement, intense competitiveness, and culture of overwork has caught many in a perfect storm of career enmeshment and burnout. Over the years, we've found that these issues interact in such complex ways with people's identity, personality, and emotions that it often requires full-on psychological therapy to address them successfully.

So, what is it about our careers that too often leads to mental health issues like those Dan faced?

**The work culture in many fields often rewards working longer hours with raises, prestige, and promotions.** Dan found that spending more and more time in the office (or tethered to his corporate iPhone) was the price he had to pay for his rise through the firm. However, when you engage in any intense activity for the great majority of your waking hours, that activity will tend to become more and more central to your identity—if only because it has displaced other activities and relationships with which you might identify.

**Certain careers or career achievements are often highly valued in an individual's family or community.** Dan's parents had both been lawyers, and while they never explicitly pushed Dan into a legal career, they had high expectations for his professional and financial achievements. When career success is seen as the ultimate life goal, individuals can feel disconnected from their family and peers if they fail to (or simply choose not to) achieve a certain level of professional success. This fear of failure and isolation drives people to center their lives on achieving what is expected of them. This intense focus and drive, however, forces their identities to ultimately become synonymous with their work.

**When jobs are paired with a big paycheck, individuals can find themselves launched into a new socioeconomic class.** It wasn't just the homes, cars, vacations, and gadgets that Dan suddenly couldn't live without—it was the friends, the dinner parties, the charity galas. Our identities are highly influenced by how we present ourselves to others. When someone forms an identity focused on wealth, achievement, and influence, they tie themselves to the high-paying career that got them there.

Even for those who don't burn out, constructing one's identity closely around a career is a risky move. Companies and entire industries struggle and go under. No matter how it happens, becoming disconnected from a career that forms the foundation of your identity can lead to bigger issues, such as depression, anxiety, substance abuse, and loneliness.

So how do you know if your identity has become enmeshed with your career? Consider the following questions:

- How much do you think about your job outside of the office? Is your mind frequently consumed with work-related thoughts? Is it difficult to participate in conversations with others that are not about your work?

- How do you describe yourself? How much of this description is tied up in your job, title, or company? Are there any other ways you would describe yourself? How quickly do you tell people you've just met about your job?

- Where do you spend most of your time? Has anyone ever complained to you that you are in the office too much?

- Do you have hobbies outside of work that do not directly involve your work-related skills and abilities? Are you able to consistently spend your time exercising other parts of your brain?

- How would you feel if you could no longer continue in your profession? How distressing would this be to you?

If these questions cause you to worry about the degree to which your job has influenced your identity, there are things you can do to initiate change. You can accomplish these on your own or with the help of a therapist who understands the challenges faced by professionals.

**Free up time.** Delegate tasks at work to free up time, and (crucially) fill that time with non-work-related activities. This could mean relying more heavily on your coworkers or advocating for an intern or additional colleague to help with tasks. Effective delegation requires giving up some control of exactly how the work is to be executed, which in itself is a healthy exercise in communication and acceptance.

**Start small.** For your new activities outside of work, start small and try out some hobbies you've had your eye on. You don't have to commit to anything long term; the idea is to start exploring new things you might want to integrate into your life and your identity. For example, if you want to exercise more, don't sign up for a marathon—just start walking to work or taking a gym break during lunch once or twice a week. Small changes like this are easier to stick with and over time can result in a virtuous cycle of improvement and commitment.

**Rebuild your network.** Reach out to friends and family to revitalize your social circles. You'll end up having fun while also establishing a support network for yourself. Even just reaching out by text, email, or phone to catch up with people you haven't spoken to in a while can help strengthen relationships. It doesn't take much; recent research on adult friendships has shown that having just three to five close friends is associated with the highest levels of life satisfaction.[1]

**Decide what's important to you.** Establish and review your principles and values. What is most important to you? Think about what you care about in life, and let those priorities guide you toward what's next. Therapists often use a process called *values clarification* to help their clients think through what matters most to them. This process involves reflecting on your desired direction in areas like relationships, community, and careers, then ranking them in terms of importance to you. While formal worksheets can be helpful, you can start by creating and updating a running list on your phone as you think about what is most important to you.

**Look beyond your job title.** Consider reframing your relationship to your career not simply in terms of your company or title, but in terms of your skills that could be used across different contexts. For example, many psychotherapists who burn out on seeing clients find that their skills translate well to human resources management or guidance counseling.

While identifying closely with your career isn't necessarily bad, it makes you vulnerable to a painful identity crisis if you burn out, get laid off, or retire. Individuals in these situations frequently suffer anxiety, depression, and despair. By claiming back some time for yourself and diversifying your activities and relationships, you can build a more balanced and robust identity in line with your values.

## QUICK RECAP

Psychologists use the term *enmeshment* to describe a situation where the boundaries between people become blurred and individual identities lose importance. Enmeshment prevents the development of a stable, independent sense of self. Enmeshment can also be applied to the boundary between self and work. While identifying closely with your career isn't necessarily bad, if you do become enmeshed with your work, it makes you vulnerable to a painful identity crisis as well as a host of other mental health issues if you burn out or get laid off.

- Becoming enmeshed in one's work can happen over time, with little awareness until it becomes problematic.

- Individuals in these situations frequently suffer anxiety, depression, burnout, loss of sense of self, and despair.

- By claiming back some time for yourself and diversifying your activities and relationships, even if in small ways, you can build a more balanced and robust identity in line with your values.

---

Adapted from "What Happens When Your Career Becomes Your Whole Identity" on hbr.org, December 26, 2019 (product #H05C4S).

Take the enmeshment self-assessment to learn whether you are at risk of becoming enmeshed with your work:

# 6

# How to Take Better Breaks at Work, According to Research

by Zhanna Lyubykh and Duygu Biricik Gulseren

For many of us, being productive means spending more time working. It seems intuitive that the more time we spend on job tasks, the more we can get done. And not surprisingly, popular literature is rife with advice on how to maximize work time. For example, the "daily routines of CEOs" often include things like waking up at 4 a.m., working on the weekend, and even being "strategic about how often you go to the bathroom." To tackle an ever-increasing workload, many workers choose to grind through, skip lunch, and stay after hours.

But the cost of being always-on (and doing it well!) is high. More than half of employees (59%) report feeling burnout, according to a recent Aflac survey.[1] Engagement has taken the opposite turn and is declining among U.S. workers.[2] Alarmingly, both high burnout and low engagement rates are associated with hindered performance. What can we do to address our declining well-being while maintaining performance?

Pausing work rather than pushing through might help with both aspects. Intrigued by two competing narratives—one focused on working more as an indicator of performance and the other on having regular respites to protect well-being—as well as mixed (and sometimes even conflicting) findings of individual studies on these topics, our team conducted a systematic review of existing research on workplace breaks.[3] In analyzing more than 80 studies, we confirmed that pausing work throughout the day can improve well-being and also help with getting more work done. Counter to the popular narrative of working long hours, our research suggests that taking breaks within work hours not only does not detract from performance, but can help boost it.

## Why Is Taking Breaks Beneficial for Well-Being and Performance?

Like batteries that need to be recharged, we all have a limited pool of physical and psychological resources. When our batteries run low, we feel depleted, exhausted, and stressed out.

Pushing through work when very little energy is left in the tank puts a strain on both well-being and work performance. In extreme cases, nonstop work can lead to a negative spiral: A worker tries to finish tasks despite their depleted state, is unable to do them well and even makes mistakes, resulting in more work and even fewer resources left to tackle those same tasks. This means that the more we work, the less productive and more exhausted we can become. Think about reading the same line for the fifth time and still not absorbing it.

The good news is that taking breaks can help employees to recharge and to short-circuit the negative spiral of exhaustion and decreasing productivity. However, not all breaks are equal in terms of their effects.

## What Types of Breaks Are More Effective for Improving Well-Being and Performance?

Breaks come in many different shapes and forms: exercising, browsing social media, going for a short walk, socializing with others, taking a nap, grabbing lunch, and so on. However, our systematic review shows that not all break types are equally effective. In other words, it matters *how* to pause work. Here are some common break elements to consider:

### Break length and timing

A longer break does not necessarily equate to a better break. Disengaging from work only for a few minutes but on a regular basis (micro-breaks) can be sufficient for preventing exhaustion and boosting performance. For example, workers can take short breaks for snacking, stretching, or simply gazing out of the window. Further, timing of the break matters—shorter breaks are more effective in the morning, while longer breaks are more beneficial in the late afternoon. This is because fatigue worsens over the workday, and we need more break time in the afternoon to recharge.

## Location of breaks

The place in which you take your breaks can make a big difference in terms of recovery. Both stretching at a desk and going outside for a short walk seem like very similar break activities, but they might substantially differ in their recharging potential. Our review demonstrates that taking a break outdoors and enjoying the green space is far better for recharging workers' resources than simply staying at a desk.

## Break activity

Engaging in physical activity during a break is effective for improving both well-being and performance. Exercising is an especially valuable recovery tool for mentally demanding work. However, the positive effects of this break type are short-lived, and employees need to exercise on a regular basis to yield its advantages.

Despite these benefits, exercise is not employees' most preferred way to spend breaks. Our review shows that browsing social media is the most common break activity—almost everyone (97%) reports engaging in it. However, researchers find that scrolling through social media during work breaks can lead to emotional exhaustion.[4] As a result, people end up with diminished creativity and work engagement instead of replenished resources—this type of break may therefore not be effective for boosting performance.

## Furry break companions

One study in our review showed that interactions with a dog can lower levels of cortisol hormone, an objective indicator of stress.[5] More research is needed in this area, as the effects on performance remain unclear. We do, however, have a strong suspicion that spending a break with a furry companion is effective for many employees. Research shows that interactions with pets can substantially boost individuals' psychological well-being, which in turn is strongly linked to performance.[6]

# What Can Managers and Organizations Do to Encourage Breaks?

The mere availability of breaks does not guarantee benefits. Workers may not use their breaks in the most efficient ways or take them at all. As decision makers and role models in organizations, managers are in an important position to encourage effective work breaks. This can be achieved in several ways.

## Fostering positive attitudes toward breaks

While employees are generally positive about breaks and report that they are beneficial for performance, this sentiment is not always shared by managers. This can deter people from recharging. It is thus critical that managers are informed about the performance-related benefits of work breaks. For example, HR managers can incorporate this information in the company's wellness training programs. Organizations can also consider implementing "wellness moments" (akin to safety moments) during which they can share their strategies for taking effective breaks and brainstorm fun break activities. Even hanging posters about the benefits of and best practices in taking breaks in the workplace can go a long way.

## Taking breaks themselves

Managers can communicate the importance of taking breaks by taking the most effective types regularly, which employees can mimic. For example, a manager who regularly walks her dog in a nearby park can communicate to her employees that she'll be stepping away from work for a bit to do so. Such strategy not only sets a positive example, but also sets clear boundaries around not interrupting breaks. Leading by example will help prevent the possible stigma and guilt associated with taking breaks. It's promising that more and more organizational leaders are recognizing this and even share their regrets about not taking sufficient time off work.[7]

## Scheduling dedicated break times

Our review shows that many employees are unable to take regular breaks or are dissuaded from doing so because of the stigma;

to address this, we recommend that managers and organizations schedule dedicated break times. These need to be implemented with care. Rigid break schedules, such as mandating that employees stop working only at a certain time and for a predetermined period, reduce employees' autonomy and can even have harmful effects. We recommend offering a total time for breaks, such as one hour a day, and leaving when and how often they want to take their breaks at the employee's discretion. Offering flexible work schedules, innovative workplace break initiatives such as "break tickets" (e.g., giving daily tickets that allow employee to take an hour of their choice off), or providing on-site social or physical activities could be some examples of optimal break scheduling.

## Creating spaces for breaks

As we highlighted above, the location of breaks can play an important role in maximizing their benefits. For example, having a small park or indoor green space can communicate the organization's commitment to facilitating work breaks and enhance the benefits of breaks in relation to employee performance. To further yield benefits of outdoor breaks, you could also make it an off-leash dog park where employees who enjoy interacting with animals can do so. This can also serve as a recruitment tool as the demand for pet-friendly workplaces is rising.[8] Many companies have already adopted pet-friendly policies.

Organizations with employees working from home can also make use of the spaces available to them by arranging online park

meetings where remote workers can join the meeting while walking or sitting at an outdoor space that is convenient to them.
Alternatively, they can allocate a "break budget" for employees
to create their own break space. For example, employees can buy
an indoor plant or a yoga mat.

. . .

Employee performance has always been a concern for organizations, and more organizations are making efforts to address
employee well-being today. Work breaks are a promising tool to
improve both. Organizations need to recognize the importance
of breaks and engage in deliberate efforts to facilitate effective
breaks.

## QUICK RECAP

Taking periodic work breaks throughout the day can boost
well-being and performance, but far too few of us take them
regularly—or take the most effective types. There are best
practices for making the most of time away from our tasks,
including where, when, and how.

- The cost of being always on is high. Engagement and well-
  being suffer when you push through instead of pausing
  work.

- Taking breaks can help employees recharge and short-
  circuit the negative spiral of exhaustion and decreasing
  productivity.

- Breaks come in different shapes and forms: exercising, browsing social media, going for a short walk, socializing with others, taking a nap, grabbing lunch, and so on.

- Break length and timing, location of breaks, and break activity all contribute to their efficacy.

- Managers and organizations should encourage their employees to take more beneficial and more frequent breaks.

---

Adapted from content posted on hbr.org,
May 31, 2023 (product #H07NKF).

# Beating Burnout

# 7

# Is Your Burnout from Too Much Work or Too Little Impact?

by Liz Wiseman

If you haven't felt it personally, you've probably heard the news: Workers are working more hours, they're exhausted, they're burned out, and they're resigning in droves.

I've been there myself. I was working at Oracle Corporation as a vice president for years in a challenging, fulfilling job when I suddenly found myself with a case of burnout. My boss urged me to take three weeks off. His instinct was good—the leisure time with my young family was refreshing. But unfortunately, the effect was ephemeral. Assuming my work was too demanding, I scaled back my responsibilities and reduced my office hours, moving to a four-day week. Yet strangely, my energy level went down, not up.

My job had become routine and perfunctory, even though I held significant management responsibility. I felt like I was turning a crank through bureaucratic sludge. And while my job performance was solid on the surface, on the inside my work felt empty. I stayed in this "easy job" for another year, assuming that a new, more challenging job would prove too consuming and prevent me from having a healthy personal and home life.

I had reconciled myself to low-grade languish until a wise friend, a dean of a medical school and a psychiatrist by training, suggested that being more deeply engaged at work might prove energy-generating, not draining, and that my feeling fulfilled would benefit my family as well. I needed my work to be meaningful and impactful.

I resigned from my job and embraced a new challenge—working as a management researcher and executive coach. At times, I worked much longer hours, but I had greater control over my work and I could see it making a difference. Once again, I was having fun and work was rewarding. I felt renewed and full of energy, which I brought home every day. Leaving my job was part of the solution, but the real, and far more sustainable, antidote to burnout was doing work that challenged me and that provided clear value to my clients.

My research studying the most influential people in the workplace, as well as my own experience, has shown me that burnout isn't necessarily a function of too much work; it's more often the result of too little impact.[1] After all, few people aspire to be job holders, but virtually everyone wants to make a difference. Here's what you can do (regardless of your level in the organization) to increase influence and impact without clocking in more hours.

## Reduce the phantom workload

Our actual workload accounts for only a portion of the burden we experience at work. More than half of respondents in one survey said that their primary source of work-related stress didn't have to do with their workload; rather, they cited stressors such as people issues, juggling work and personal lives, and lack of job security.[2] Workplace politics and drama create friction, and complex collaborations and endless meetings take up time. Another study found that U.S. employees spend on average 2.8 hours per week dealing with workplace conflicts.[3] These factors constitute a phantom workload and exacerbate burnout.

You can help make work lighter for yourself and others by eschewing politics and drama, being easy to work with. How?

We all know coworkers who create a tax. They may not actively foment conflict; they simply contribute to the stress by participating in the clatter on the periphery of the actual work and adding to the noise. Then there are the colleagues who provide a time rebate because they are, simply put, easy to work with. The work doesn't necessarily become easier, but the process of working becomes easier and more enjoyable. They provide lift and foster a light environment that lowers stress and increases the joy of work, both of which reduce burnout. So find your way to a team of people who make work easier and who steer clear of drama. That's the easiest place to start.

## Increase the level of challenge (not the volume) of work

My research surveying professionals across a variety of industries revealed a strong correlation between "challenge level" and "satisfaction level" at work, meaning that as the degree of challenge in one's work increases, so does job satisfaction.[4] However, the data also showed that when a job involves the highest degree of challenge, job satisfaction plateaus, which means there's a sweet spot where challenge is present but manageable. Make sure you get a steady diet of meaningful challenges—projects with visible impact and a scope that will invite you to stretch but won't leave you strung out.

If you want to dial up the challenge level without burning out, look for ways to flex your job scope. Treat your job description less like a boundary that restricts your movement and more like a base camp from which you spot critical problems and pursue opportunities to make an important contribution. You can also try practicing what I call the "naive yes" by agreeing to a new challenge before your brain kicks in and tells you it's not possible. As Richard Branson said, "If somebody offers you an amazing opportunity but you are not sure you can do it, say yes—then learn how to do it later!" Of course, don't say yes to everything; say yes to challenges that are a size too big, and then grow into them.

## Negotiate the nontangibles necessary for success

When working on difficult projects fraught with unforeseen obstacles, we often assume that we need additional resources (such as budget or headcount) to complete the work; however, in reality, our most vital resources are less tangible. In surveying professionals from various industries about the resources they most need to be successful, these six factors were rated of similarly high importance: (1) access to information, (2) action from leaders,

(3) feedback or coaching, (4) access to key meetings and people, (5) time, and (6) help establishing credibility. However, across all industries, countries, and demographics, one thing was consistent: budget and headcount were rated in seventh and eighth place—the least important factors by a significant margin. You don't need resources as much as managerial support and aircover.

You can increase your impact by negotiating for the guidance, coaching, and sponsorship you'll need beforehand. For example, as a relatively young manager at Oracle, I had an opportunity to work with the company's three top executives on a highly visible leadership development program that would roll out over the coming year. These executives were all-in as we developed and ran the first session. It was a resounding success, but I was concerned that these busy execs would get pulled away and I would be left to carry on the program without executive support. When we met to plan the next session, I decided to speak up. I assured the president that I would give this my all, but I couldn't be successful without his ongoing, active involvement. I said, "If you stop working on this, I'll have to stop too." The president paused to consider my bold request and then resolutely said, "You have a deal." He called to his executive assistant, "For the next year, Liz has whatever time she needs on my calendar." He remained fully engaged, and our work was deeply impactful and a richly fulfilling experience for me.

## Share the leadership load

Cross-functional collaboration requires contributors and managers across organizations to be willing to take on extra leadership roles. But when the same people are continually tapped to lead, those summoned for extra leadership duties wind up chronically overworked while others become underutilized. Both conditions lead to burnout.

Increasingly, organizations are adopting a more fluid approach to leadership, one that looks less like a pride of lions and more like a flock of geese. A flock of migrating geese flies in a distinctive V formation, which scientists estimate enables the flock to travel 71% farther in a given period than solo flight. In this formation, the bird in the front of the flock breaks the air, reducing drag for the birds flying behind. Eventually, the lead bird tires, falls back into the formation, and another bird rotates to take its turn in the lead.

If you are new to the workforce, don't wait to be promoted into a managerial role before you take on leadership roles. You can volunteer to lead an initiative or look for leadership vacuums in everyday moments and then step in to fill the void. If you're in a meeting that lacks a clear leader—offer to facilitate the discussion. Or if the agenda is unclear, you might simply ask, "What is the most important thing for us to accomplish during this meeting?" When team members can step in and out of leadership roles with equal ease, each member of the team has an opportunity to play a major role and the entire team experiences less fatigue.

## Avoid reckless persistence

A dogged determination to finish everything we start can lead to misplaced energy and wasted resources. A friend of mine once half-jokingly remarked that he finally stopped dating a woman when he realized he was spending all his time with someone else's future wife. Similarly, when we can't let go of unproductive projects before they finish, we can rob our organization of the time and resources needed to pursue higher-value opportunities. Furthermore, finishing for the sake of finishing can result in a Pyrrhic victory in which success inflicts such heavy tolls on the winners (and their teams) that the victory is indistinguishable from defeat. In the wake of these battles lie exhausted, alienated colleagues who become reluctant to join the next campaign, and burnout abounds.

Instead of finishing at all costs, you might need to cut your losses and let some projects go. If you suspect you are engaged in an unwinnable battle or working on yesterday's priorities, ask yourself: (1) Is this still relevant, given changes in the larger environment or market? (2) Is this still important to the organization and my leadership? (3) Is this something we can still be successful at, even if we don't finish? If the answers are "no," it might be time to let it go. But don't abandon the work without getting clearance from your leader(s) or stakeholders, and be sure to let them know what you will do instead to provide greater value— or let them direct you as you pivot to a higher-priority project.

. . .

Our work, both the real work and the phantom workload, can feel inescapable and exhausting. Offering (and taking) much-needed R&R is a good start, but the solution may not be working less, it might be taking more control and achieving greater impact in the work we are doing. We need to look beyond the *where* and *when* of the workplace and focus on the *what* and *why* of the work. When we increase our impact per workhour, we can rekindle that fire in our bellies. And when work is a build-up experience, not a burnout experience, we feel a sense of fulfillment and purpose that feeds our souls.

## QUICK RECAP

When it comes to burnout, it's natural to assume that by lessening our workload we can fight the culprit. But burnout isn't necessarily a function of too much work; it is more often the result of too little impact. Try increasing your impact without adding more hours.

- Reduce the phantom workload. Work-related stress doesn't just come from the amount of work you do.

- Increase the level of the challenge (not the volume) of the work. Find projects with visible impact and a scope that will invite you to stretch yourself.

- Share the leadership load. If you are new to the workforce, don't wait to be promoted into a managerial role before you take on leadership roles.

Adapted from content posted on hbr.org,
December 10, 2021 (product #H06QY3).

# 8

# Battle Burnout with This Acronym

by Carson Tate

The days blur together, your eyedrops no longer help with Zoom fatigue, and the thought of opening the pigsty that is masquerading as your inbox makes you want to scream.

Overwhelmed, overstretched, and just entirely over it, in the last year, seven in 10 workers have experienced burnout.[1]

The World Health Organization recognized burnout as an official occupational syndrome back in 2019.[2] It's defined as the result of chronic workplace stress and characterized by three things:

- Feelings of energy depletion or exhaustion

- Increased mental distance from or cynicism about your job

- Reduced professional efficacy (i.e., you're unproductive)

Burnout is an organizational issue—meaning we, as employees, are not responsible for solving it. Still, it is not entirely out of our control. We can choose to set boundaries that protect our mental, physical, and emotional health. The challenge is that our efforts to do so are often hijacked by guilt.

Will our boss be upset if we don't respond to their 9 p.m. Slack? Will we look lazy and selfish if we don't put in a 60-hour week? Will our team members think we're unmotivated if we take a full hour for lunch?

Questions like these make us feel like we should always be giving more, doing the most, and working harder. We are driven by the guilt we might feel if we put our personal needs first or the fear of disappointing others.

But at what cost?

When we are given a choice, and we still select our jobs over what our bodies and minds need—real breaks, time with loved ones, and empty space to rest and think—we end up letting the most important person down: our self.

That's why it's important to learn how to say no to the voices in your head and start making choices that give you the energy to do your best work. Before you respond to the next request for your time or talents, use this acronym to E.M.P.O.W.E.R. your decisions by taking the steps outlined below.

## Evaluate

When your face turns red and it feels as if your head is going to explode from one more request for your time and talents, take a breath and evaluate the facts. Remember, a fact is an actual occurrence. It is something that can be proven through observation or measurement. What are the facts of the request? How much time is required? How much preparation is necessary? Get the data.

For example, let's say your boss sends you a Slack at 9 p.m. on Tuesday and asks you to join her at a new hire recruiting event the following Monday night. Before responding, consider the facts of her request. The event starts at 6:00 p.m. in the lobby of your office building and ends at 7:30 p.m. You do not need to prepare for the event, so your total time investment would be 90 minutes.

## My story

What is the story you are telling yourself about this request? A story is a judgment or assumption you use to make sense of why you are being asked to contribute to yet another project or event. When we are burned out, we often assign motives to the people asking for more of our time to explain the logic behind their actions. However, stories are usually inaccurate, because they are driven by our subjective emotions. To make the best decision, you need to separate feelings from facts.

Sticking with our original example, you might tell yourself the story, "Of course my boss sent this Slack now! She doesn't respect work-life boundaries because she expects everyone to be available and work 24/7, like she does." To separate the facts from your feelings, re-read the message your boss sent. Did she ask you to respond immediately? Or are you making assumptions driven by your own anxieties? It's important to debunk any false narrative you may be telling yourself so that you can take the time to consider your response thoughtfully.

## Priorities

Once you're clear on what's fact and what's fiction, you're ready to consider whether it's worthwhile to take on a new request. At this point, that guilt-driven voice in your head may jump in to tell you that, yes, you should absolutely do it. Don't listen. Instead, stop and evaluate the priority of the task you are being asked to do. How does this ask for your time align with your responsibilities, the organization's strategic goals, and/or your personal needs?

In the case of the 9 p.m. Slack request, at this point, you want to determine if the new hire recruiting event aligns with one of the organization's strategic goals as well as your professional goals. For example, if your company is trying to recruit and hire 20 new analysts this year and one of your professional priorities is to build relationships with leaders throughout the company, you may want to attend. However, if you're more focused on building your skills as an individual contributor and believe that these extra hours will be more draining than energizing, you should probably turn your boss down.

## Opportunities

Next, take it a step further and think about the opportunities that you may gain from taking on or turning down the request. Ask: *What doors will this request open for me if I participate? Will it enable me to advance in my career, develop a new skill, or build new relationships? Or is it illuminating something that requires additional attention in my personal life?*

For instance, if you were to attend the new hire recruiting event, you could strengthen your networking skills and meet leaders from all divisions in the organization. But if you were to decline, you might have a relaxing night with your friends and do an even better job on a project that is aligned with the skills and capabilities you want to develop. Weigh the cost-benefit of each decision and choose the one that aligns with the goals that are most important to you.

## Who

Who made the ask? What is your relationship to this person? What's at stake in the relationship if you say yes or if you say no? Answering these questions will help you figure out how to best frame your response should it be no.

If your manager is making a request, as in the recruiting event example, and you decide to turn it down, you may need to discuss your decision with her. This will allow you to explain yourself and set healthy boundaries without appearing dismissive of her ask.

You might say, "I appreciate the invitation to attend the new hire event. I have three projects due later this week and was going to use this time to prepare. I'd like to explore how I can support you and the company without attending the event. Would you be open to that?"

On the other hand, if a request is coming from a peer or work friend, the stakes may be lower, and you can respectfully explain why you are declining without a further conversation.

## Expectations

Expectations are the guiding principles and ideologies we use to inform our decision making, and they often lie just below the surface of our awareness. Ask yourself: *Whose standards are influencing my decision to say yes or no? What does the person making the request expect of me, and have they clearly set those expectations?* The goal is to clarify and decouple your expectations from the expectations of the people in your life.

For example, if you know your manager expects her team members to be visible at corporate events, this might change how you respond to her request. However, if you realize that you are the one setting unrealistic expectations for yourself, you may feel more comfortable and confident in your decision to decline.

## Real

We all have the same 168 hours in a week. Every time you say yes to something, you are saying no to something else. Get real about the implications of your decision. What is the best and worst thing that could happen if you said yes or no? This is an essential final step to ensure you thoughtfully considered the positive and negative implications the decision will have on your time and energy.

If you say yes to attending the new hire event, the best thing that may happen is you assist your career advancement. If you say no, the worst thing that might happen is your manager could question your allegiance—but remember, there are also ways to clarify your decision and potentially avoid this outcome. In the end, it's your choice, and you ought to set boundaries that feel right and good to you.

. . .

Guilt and "shoulds" lead us to overcommit—and when you overcommit, the quality of your work and life suffers. Avoid bankrupting your life. Stop the "shoulds" from undermining your decisions and E.M.P.O.W.E.R. your choices, starting today.

## QUICK RECAP

Burnout is an organizational issue. Employees are not responsible for solving it. Still, we can choose to set boundaries that protect our mental, physical, and emotional health. Before you respond to the next request for your time or talents, use this acronym to E.M.P.O.W.E.R. your decisions.

- **Evaluate.** The next time someone asks you for your time or talents, take a deep breath, and evaluate the facts.

- **My story.** What story are you telling yourself? We often assign motives to the people asking for our time to explain the logic behind their actions. Separate feelings from facts.

- **Priorities.** Stop and evaluate the priority of the task you are being asked to do.

- **Opportunities.** Think about the opportunities that you may gain from taking on, or turning down, the request.

- **Who.** Who made the ask? What's at stake if you say yes—or no? Answering these questions will help you figure out how to best frame your response.

- **Expectations.** Whose standards are influencing your decision to say yes, or no? The goal is to clarify and decouple your expectations from those of the person asking for your time.

- **Real.** Every time you say yes to something you are saying no to something else. Get real about the implications of your decision.

---

Adapted from content posted on hbr.org,
June 25, 2021 (product #H06FZ9).

# 9

# Is Your Job Stress Perceived or Circumstantial?

by Brendan P. Keegan

Recently, I went out to dinner at a local restaurant. It was clear our server had too many tables and was struggling to keep up with all of them. Whether this was due to a labor shortage or one of his coworkers calling in sick, it occurred to me that, on this particular day, his job was more stressful than mine.

It made me grateful for the day of work I'd had (even though it had felt like a stressful one before I met our server), and it changed my perspective.

We all complain about job stress—according to Gallup's *State of the Global Workplace* report, stress among the world's workers reached an all-time high in 2021.[1] And some jobs are legitimately stressful—think paramedics, firefighters, nurses, social workers, and others who respond to emergency situations.

But the experience with my server made me think about the role my own perception plays in my stress levels. Clinical psychologist Richard Lazarus asserts that work stress isn't solely about the situation or the person. Rather, it's about how the situation and person interact.[2]

For example, let's say you're a warehouse inventory specialist or sales associate, and one of the people who typically helps your team process orders for customers calls in sick. The fact that you have to pick up the slack and handle more orders faster than usual can shift your perception to see your job as more stressful because you're comparing your new workload to what you're used to. Your stress level also might go up as you worry about meeting the new expectations that resulted from your team member's absence.

While you can't change the situation that's causing you stress, the good news is that you can manage your perception of it by examining and intentionally challenging how you see your job. Here are three ways to reframe your outlook:

## Examine whether you have realistic expectations

We all have expectations that add to our stress and perception of how hard our job is. Consider working from home versus working in the office. A person working from home might perceive that their job is more stressful because they are more isolated and spend the time they would have used for a commute to do more work tasks. A person working in the office might perceive their job as more stressful because they think the person working from home has more flexibility and doesn't have to deal with a daily commute. Similarly, suppose employees typically finish a given task in eight hours. A worker might feel stressed if the job takes them closer to 10 hours to complete because of their own pace.

The first thing to do is look for the source of your expectations. Where did they originate? What molded them? Understanding this can help you pause and consciously challenge your views and the feelings—including stress—that come from them.

I'll always remember the very first day of my career when the president of the company said it's not the best employee that gets promoted, it's the best-known employee. I was taken aback. That's not what I had been taught. But I stopped to think about why it went against my expectations. Factors like my childhood, education, and background all likely colored what I believed. That didn't mean what I believed was wrong, but it also didn't mean that my president was wrong. He'd had his own business experiences that led him to think about promotions in a different way, and at the time, he'd had much more of that kind of experience than I had. So, instead of being disappointed in the fact that my expectations weren't met, I chose to acknowledge my president's perspective. It's stuck with me ever since.

## Talk to colleagues who seem to manage their stress

To set more realistic expectations, you can ask those around you to help you recalibrate. Start by finding people who seem to cope well. Ask if they'd be willing to share whatever thoughts, mindsets, or strategies help them manage expectations and stay positive when they aren't met.

For example, you can ask these coworkers who seem to be coping well if you can shadow them for a few hours. Job shadowing enables you to observe how others work and consider new approaches that you might not have thought of. You might be able to implement new positive habits or practices you see, such as taking more frequent breaks, developing templates, or applying more effective operational models, into your own work. Shadowing also helps you make more realistic comparisons of what you face compared to everyone else, because you witness firsthand what others go through instead of basing everything on assumptions, thereby removing unrealistic expectations of those you work with and your own job.

Importantly, there's no exact formula for what will relieve stress for someone. If someone else's method doesn't work for or appeal to you, that's OK. The point is just to collect some recommendations and expose yourself to potential solutions to try.

## Practice gratitude and strengthen relationships

Our brains are hard-wired to see the negative around us to help us stay safe and avoid problems. Over time, however, it's easy for us to nitpick and find every little wrong thing. Intentionally practicing gratitude gradually trains your brain to see more of the good in your work, making your view of the job more balanced and accurate. With that balance, you might be able to reduce your stress level.

Try taking a few minutes before starting your workday to note what you're excited to do and what you're thankful for. This could be as simple as being thankful for the great coffee or how short your commute time is.

As you work on your gratitude practice, consider the other people around you. If you're thankful for something they've said or done, tell them so. Reaching out like this can have a powerful influence and strengthen your relationships, and strong relationships have a protective effect on well-being. One study showed that in the United States, higher relationship quality decreases the likelihood that stressors, when present, will result in depressive symptoms.[3] Taking this effect into account, when workers feel better, they also usually are able to handle a better variety of tasks on the job. That ability to tackle responsibilities safely and well can influence how employees perceive their role.

. . .

When thinking about your work stress levels, it can be tempting to assume the grass is greener for people in other positions. The reality, however, is that jobs aren't harder or easier—they're just different. Whether or not your job adds undue stress may be a personal perception. The pressures of a job may color how you experience the position, but remember that you are not powerless in your ability to manage them.

## QUICK RECAP

Work stress isn't solely about the situation or the person. Rather, it's about how the situation and person interact. While you can't always change the situation that's causing you

stress, the good news is that you can manage your perception of it by examining and intentionally challenging how you
see your job.

- Examine if you have realistic expectations, then pause
  and consciously challenge your views and the feelings—
  including stress—that come from them.

- Talk to colleagues who seem to be managing their stress
  well.

- Practice gratitude and strengthen your relationships.

---

Adapted from content posted on hbr.org,
February 1, 2023 (product #H07F4M).

# 10

# Three Types of Burnout, and How to Overcome Them

by Melody Wilding

Take a moment to imagine a person who's burned out. You're likely picturing someone who is overbooked and overwhelmed, drowning in multiple demands and competing priorities.

But burnout is far more nuanced than simply being busy and tired.

For years, it was believed that everyone reacted to chronic workplace stress in the same way. But research has revealed that burnout manifests itself in different ways depending on a person's work environment as well as their internal resources, including dedication to their job and coping mechanisms.[1]

Let's take a closer look at the three types of burnout and how you can overcome each one.

# Overload Burnout

*Overload burnout* occurs when you work harder and more frantically to achieve success, often to the detriment of your health and personal life. This is the type of burnout that most people are familiar with, and it's also the most common.

Overload burnout typically affects highly dedicated employees who feel obligated to work at an unsustainable pace. As a result, they drive themselves to the point of physical and mental exhaustion.

Professionals with overload burnout tend to cope by venting their emotions to others (e.g., complaining about how tired and overwhelmed they are). This subtype is also quick to jump into problem-solving mode, creating more work and responsibility for themselves, which only exacerbates their stress.

## Signs to watch out for

- You overlook your own needs or personal life to fulfill work demands.

- You invest more than is healthy in your commitment to your career or ambitions.

- You endanger your well-being to achieve your goals.

## How to address it

Researchers note that the way out of overload burnout is two-fold. First, it's important to develop stronger emotion-regulation skills, such as naming and processing your emotions and reframing negative self-talk. For instance, you could reframe the belief that you need to work all the time to be successful to "enjoying my life helps me become more successful." After all, resting is not a reward for success. It's a prerequisite for performance.

Second, it's crucial to separate your self-worth from your work. "Consequently, by learning to keep a certain distance from work," researchers Jesús Montero-Marín and Javier García-Campayo write, ". . . individuals could avoid excessive involvement and prevent burnout."[2]

Strive to diversify your identity—to create self-complexity— by investing in different areas of your life beyond work. You might decide to devote time to your role as a spouse, parent, or friend. During the pandemic, one of my clients restored an old identity by renewing his pilot's license. Volunteering with the Civil Air Patrol proved to be a healthy forcing function to get away from his computer, while also contributing to his sense of well-being.

## Under-Challenged Burnout

You might be surprised to find out that burnout can result from doing too little. *Under-challenged burnout* could be considered the opposite of the overload subtype. It occurs when you're bored and not stimulated by your job, which leads to a lack of motivation. People with under-challenged burnout may feel underappreciated and become frustrated because their role lacks learning opportunities, room for growth, or meaningful connection with coworkers and leadership.

Workers who feel their tasks are monotonous and unfulfilling tend to lose passion and become cynical and lethargic. They cope with the stress of being under-challenged through avoidance—distraction, dissociation, or thought suppression (e.g., ordering themselves to "stop thinking about that").

## Signs to watch out for

- You would like to work on assignments and tasks that are more challenging.

- You feel your job does not offer you opportunities to develop your abilities.

- You feel that your current role is hampering your ability to advance and develop your talents.

## How to address it

When you're demoralized, it can be hard to care about much of anything. Lower the stakes by simply exploring your curiosities. Set a goal to learn a new skill in the next 30 days to kick-start your motivation. Start small and don't overwhelm yourself. Perhaps you spend an hour or two a week learning to code or devote 20 minutes a day practicing a new language.

Making strides toward something that feels fun and meaningful to you creates a flywheel of momentum that can lift you out of a funk. Even if the skill isn't directly related to your job, you'll likely find that the positive energy spills over to reinvigorate your passion for your work—or that it inspires your career to move in a new direction.

You might also try job crafting to turn the job you have into the one you want. Again, baby steps are key. Focusing on incremental changes can add up to big results. Take my client Alice, a product management lead. As the pandemic wore on, she increasingly felt under-challenged by her role, which mostly comprised team performance management. So I gave her an assignment. For two weeks, she tracked what tasks created the most psychological flow. A clear pattern emerged: Talking to customers lit her up, as did solving challenging workflow problems. Alice's manager was ecstatic when she proposed a new research project combining those skill sets to innovate the company's core product.

## Neglect Burnout

The final type of burnout is the worn-out subtype. This is also called *neglect burnout*, because it can result from feeling helpless in the face of challenges. Neglect burnout occurs when you aren't given enough structure, direction, or guidance in the workplace. You may find it difficult to keep up with demands or otherwise feel unable to meet expectations. Over time, this can make you feel incompetent, frustrated, and uncertain.

The worn-out worker copes through learned helplessness, which occurs when a person feels unable to find solutions to difficult situations—even when some are available. In other words, people with learned helplessness tend to feel incapable of making any positive difference in their circumstances. When things at work don't turn out as they should, those with neglect burnout become passive and stop trying.

## Signs to watch out for

- You stop trying when work situations don't go as planned.

- You give up in response to obstacles or setbacks you face at work.

- You feel demoralized when you get up in the morning and have to face another day at work.

## How to address it

Find ways to regain a sense of agency over your role. Try creating a to-don't list. What can you get off your plate by outsourcing, delegating, or delaying? Look for tasks you need to say no to altogether and hone the skill of setting stronger boundaries. A great place to start is by identifying situations where you feel an intense sense of resentment. This is an emotional signal that you need to put healthier limits in place.

Likewise, consider talking to your boss about your workload. You could explain how you're currently spending your time and ask, "Are my priorities consistent with yours? What would you like me to change?" or "If we could take Project A off of my plate, then I'd have more time to focus on our team's strategic priorities and ultimately deliver on the key goals we've evaluated against." Your manager will likely be thrilled you're thinking about the big picture and taking initiative.

Most importantly, focus on what you can control. Outside of office hours, be bullish about self-care. Create routines and rituals that ground you, such as a daily walk or journaling practice. When you feel helpless about changing tides at work, some semblance of predictability is essential.

. . .

Because people don't burn out in the exact same way or for the exact same reasons, it's important to identify the type of burnout that you may be facing. You may even be dealing with a mix of one or two of these types at the same time. Determining where you're at makes it easier to find targeted solutions to solve the specific challenges ahead of you.

## QUICK RECAP

People don't burn out in the same way or for the same reasons. So it's important to identify the type of burnout that you may be facing. You may even be dealing with a mix of one or two of these types at the same time.

- Overload burnout occurs when you work harder and more frantically to achieve success, often to the detriment of your health and personal life.

- Under-challenged burnout can result from doing too little.

- Neglect burnout can result from feeling helpless in the face of challenges.

- Each type of burnout has its own signs to watch out for and ways to overcome it.

---

Adapted from "3 Types of Burnout, and How to Overcome Them" on hbr.org, August 22, 2022 (product #H0773Z).

# Make Your To-Do List Work for You

# 11

# How to Say No to Extra Work

by Vasundhara Sawhney

Consider an average workday. How many of your tasks fit perfectly into your job description?

I'll go first.

As an editor, my core responsibilities include writing and editing, analyzing business research and trends, thinking about our longer-term content strategy, and commissioning new authors from around the world. What do I typically do all day? Apart from my core tasks, I help colleagues write critical emails to clients. I review marketing materials for upcoming projects or events. I sit in on business strategy meetings. I mentor interns. I sometimes work on cross-functional teams that need editorial expertise. Occasionally, I plan office get-togethers or team-building activities. None of these noncore activities are a part of my job description.

I often don't mind doing additional work, especially if it contributes to organizational goals in a meaningful way. But once in a while, even when the work is interesting or opens the door to new opportunities, I just don't have enough bandwidth or mental space to take it on. Can you relate?

In these situations, there is a right and wrong way to turn down tasks—whether the person prompting you is your boss, your colleague, or your peer. Instead of pushing back or going on the defensive, you can be thoughtful, explain your reasoning, and avoid making enemies along the way. This is a critical skill, especially for new workers who may lack the experience, confidence, or vocabulary to say no, and often end up burned out and overworked as a result.

If you struggle to say no at work, here is some sample language to help you.

## Reason it out

New at work? Be careful about how you turn your colleagues down. People haven't had an opportunity to get to know you yet, and they may make negative assumptions about your personality or work ethic if you respond to their request with a straightforward "no." Protect your reputation by giving them a clear reason why you think you can't take on the task.

> *Instead of saying:* "Karla, you've asked me to take on a new project, but I have way too much work already. I can't do it. Sorry about that."

> *Try:* "Karla, with my current workload, I don't think I'll be able to meet the expectations you have for this project. If you feel I'm the best person for the job, I'd love to sit down with you and reassess my current schedule and priorities."

## Be diplomatic but truthful

Sometimes we overbook ourselves without realizing that there could be a conflict in the future. Maybe you said yes to an exciting opportunity a few months ago, but didn't account for other professional commitments that would need more of your time. Or maybe you didn't anticipate another project would get extended. Uncommitting is hard but should be done gracefully. Aim to be clear, assertive, and above all, thoughtful.

> *Instead of saying:* "Zahir, I know I said yes to being on the committee, but I'm sorry. I don't think I can do this right now. I've got too many other things happening."

> *Try:* "When I said I could join the committee last month, I fully believed I had enough bandwidth to do a great job. After taking a closer look at my calendar, I realized I've overextended myself and there are several professional commitments I can't move. This means I won't be able to participate. I still think it's a great opportunity and would love to participate in the future."

## Reframe the opportunity

There are times when we have to call in sick or take time off for personal emergencies. The same is true of our colleagues. When this happens, you may be asked to help accommodate the situation by taking on a few extra tasks. If you find yourself in a situation where you're being asked to cover for a peer and you don't have the experience or skills to handle the request quickly and confidently, don't immediately turn it down. "No" should be reserved for things that cannot be done under any circumstances.

Consider whether you may be tempted to turn the task down out of fear; if this is the case, try reframing it as a development opportunity.

> *Instead of saying:* "Sorry, that's outside my skill set. I won't be able to deliver the results you want."

> *Try:* "This kind of work is still new to me, but if you accept that I'd need a little extra time to tackle the learning curve, then I'd love to take a crack at it."

## Explain why it's in everyone's best interest

Sometimes you might be presented with cross-functional opportunities—chances to work with other teams—that can help you gain a better understanding of other parts of the business. If you want to be a manager, these opportunities can help you build skills and relationships that may help you advance your career. This work can be difficult to turn down. But you need to think of how saying yes might impact you and your team. If an assignment would detract from your core responsibilities or would compromise your ability to consistently deliver high-quality work without the significant upside of learning or relationship building, it's probably best to decline.

> *Instead of saying:* "Sorry, this isn't in my job description, and I have too much on my plate right now."

*Try:* "That sounds like a great opportunity. But we're a small team. If I devoted five hours a week to marketing activities, then we might be scrambling on our key product launch dates and my team would suffer. Thank you for thinking of me. I'd love to learn more about marketing. And I hope you'll consider me when another opportunity arises."

## QUICK RECAP

You won't always have enough bandwidth or mental space to take on additional work. In these situations, there is a right and wrong way to turn down tasks—whether the person prompting you is your boss, your colleague, or your peer.

- Instead of pushing back or going on the defensive, you can be thoughtful, explain your reasoning, and avoid making enemies along the way.

- Be diplomatic but truthful. Uncommitting is hard but should be done gracefully. Aim to be clear, assertive, and above all, thoughtful.

- Reframe the task as a development opportunity but set expectations from the start.

- Explain why it's in everyone's best interest for you to decline an opportunity.

Adapted from "Work Speak: How to Say 'No' to Extra Work" on hbr.org, April 19, 2023 (product #H07LP0).

Wondering how to say no to a not-so-great request from your boss? Watch this video to learn how:

# 12

# Stop Trying to Manage Your Time

## by Amantha Imber

For all of us, 2020 was quite the year, but for Adore Beauty cofounder Kate Morris, work was particularly stressful. Not only was she managing one of the largest online retail businesses in Australia through a pandemic, but she was also preparing to list her company on the Australian Stock Exchange.

"I remember looking at the schedule our bankers had created," Morris told me. "I said to them, 'There must be a mistake, because you have me on back-to-back Zoom calls for 12 hours every day for weeks.' They just nodded and said it was a standard roadshow."

Morris knew then that the key to making it through this period with her mental health intact would be managing her energy—her time was already spoken for.

Her business coach advised her to return to her purpose. What did she really want to achieve with this IPO? The answer was clear: She wanted it to be the largest-ever IPO in Australia led by a female founder and a female CEO. For Morris, it was about making history.

Morris's coach encouraged her to write this down in a place where she could see it *loud and clear*. "I put it on a sticky note on the bottom of my computer monitor since I was going to be staring at it for 12 hours a day. The note said: *'Making history.'*"

Even when she was delivering the exact same presentation for the nth time on a given day, seeing those words reminded Morris why she was doing it. "It helped me make every presentation fresh—like I was giving it for the first time."

This is just one of the many energy management tips I've learned while interviewing people for my podcast: If you feel like you're flailing, connect with your purpose. This might be your overall career purpose (why you have chosen the profession that you are in) or a micro purpose (what is motivating you to do a great job on a project or task). But don't stop there. Write down your purpose and keep it on your desk to act as a constant visual reminder of why you do what you do, especially when things are exhausting or stressful.

That note may give you the boost you need to get through the day.

If you want a few more tips, here are more pieces of advice that I've learned from my guests to help you spring back up when your energy is low.

## Create a "wall of encouragement"

Despite having competed in several marathons and Ironman competitions over the course of her life, Fulbright scholar, writer, and

CEO Holly Ransom spends a lot of time sitting at her desk. For someone used to running many miles each week, the stagnation is agonizing. To help manage her restless energy over the course of the pandemic, during which she spent over 250 days in lockdown in Melbourne, Ransom created a wall of encouragement.

In her home office, Ransom lined the windowsill with cards that the most important people in her life had sent her over the years. "They have messages of support. There are probably a couple of times a week when I inadvertently read one or two, but sometimes I'll do it intentionally."

The cards remind Ransom of why she does what she does every day. They reenergize her when she's feeling drained and help her overcome something we all deal with: *negativity bias*— our propensity to place more emphasis on negative information than positive. Humans are basically suckers for punishment, and when we experience setbacks or receive negative feedback at work, it has a big impact on our energy levels.

In your own workspace, think about how you can create a wall of encouragement. It might be physical, like Ransom's, or it might be digital, like a folder on your desktop that contains encouraging emails, awards, positive feedback, or even memes that make you laugh. Social scientists have found that inducing a positive mood has many benefits, including improved well-being and general happiness.[1]

## Remove recurring irritants

In his bestselling book *Upstream*, Dan Heath wrote about a regular annoyance that used to happen in his life. Heath spends a lot of time writing in cafes and a part of this ritual involves fishing his power cord out of his bag, plugging it into the wall, and then, when he returns to his office, digging the power cord out again, plugging it into the wall again, and so on.

"I've got a hundred cords around my desk. So, it's always just a little bit of a nuisance. But it just seemed like one of those things—that's the way it had to be," he said.[2]

In the process of writing *Upstream*, Heath began thinking about how to better solve problems by targeting their root cause. It suddenly occurred to him that he could save himself time and frustrated energy just by buying a second power cord to live in his laptop bag and keeping the original cord at his office.

The solution was so simple. Why did it take writing a book on problem-solving to figure it out?

Heath told me it's because of a force called *tunneling*, coined by Eldar Shafir and Sendhil Mullainathan. When we have limited cognitive resources (or brain power) due to life stresses, we adopt tunnel vision and miss opportunities to identify and solve problems. Particularly when we are dealing with one or two big issues (like a global pandemic), our brain power diminishes and we have less mental capacity to deal with other things.

In the context of the power cord problem, we can look at it like this: When we are facing several big problems in our lives, we ironically don't have the capacity to solve the little one. As a result, we tend to engage in short-term, reactive thinking.

To escape the trap of tunneling, give yourself some slack in the form of time or resources. For example, is there a simple process that you find yourself executing regularly (budgeting, paying bills) that could be automated using software? Are there standard emails that you find yourself writing again and again that you could create a template for?

All of these small tasks eat away at your energy. Finding and eliminating these recurring irritants will help free up the time and resources you need to deal with the bigger things in your life.

## Create a "to-don't" list

Rachel Botsman is a world-renowned expert on trust and technology and a Trust Fellow at Oxford University. Prior to the pandemic, Botsman had written an annual "to-don't" list for several years. The purpose of the list was to reflect on things she wanted to do differently. But during her first Covid lockdown, she made this ritual monthly.

"So much of our lives are programmed to *add* tasks and commitments," Botsman told me. "We're not taught how to *subtract* or take things away."

To overcome the feeling of the never-ending to-do list, Botsman has an ongoing appointment with herself on the last Friday of every month, when she sets aside time to consider what she wants to stop doing in her work.

"I give myself a full hour to think about it and reflect on the last month's list. What did I keep? What did I find hard? Why? What is a pattern I can break?" This process has made Botsman more mindful about where she puts her energy and helps her focus on the work that matters most.

When thinking about your "to-don't" list, consider the things you're currently doing that are sucking up your energy. There might be certain people that you decide *not* to see, certain habits that you want to break, or projects that are no longer serving your growth at work. Sadly, there may also be a few items that you *want* to drop but can't at this stage in your career. Don't dwell on them; focus instead on the things that are in your control.

. . .

With the rising demands of our workplaces and the endless things that *have* to get done, we may not always be able to manage our time. Time is a finite resource, and it can't be flexed. But energy is not. Use the strategies highlighted above to protect your well-being and give yourself the spark you need when you're feeling down.

## QUICK RECAP

With the rising demands of our workplaces and the endless things to get done, we may not always be able to manage our time. Time is a finite resource, and it can't be flexed. But energy is not. There are ways to give yourself the spark you need when you're feeling down.

- Put your purpose on a sticky note. Keep it at your desk to act as a constant visual reminder of why you do what you do.

- Create "a wall of encouragement" to look at when you need to feel reenergized or are feeling drained.

- Eliminate tasks you do regularly that eat away at your energy level.

- Create a "to-don't" list of things that no longer serve your growth at work.

---

Adapted from content posted on hbr.org,
April 4, 2022 (product #H06YM5).

# 13

# Three Practical Ways to Be More Productive

by Ian Daley

Early in my corporate career, I was masterful at replying to emails instantly and staying on top of the multitude of requests I received from colleagues, vendors—and truthfully—anyone with my email address. There was an odd satisfaction in powering through my inbox. I felt entirely in control.

It was 2009, and as a newly minted pharmaceutical sales rep, I believed this attitude was a marker of success. To some degree, it served me well. I was highly attentive to customers, viewed as reliable by my team, and could deliver on any ad hoc requests from the head office.

My success fed my false belief that when something works once, it will work again and again. As a recent grad, at the start of my career, it was easy to fall prey to this thinking. I had hit a home run in my first at-bat. It wasn't until a few years later, when I was offered a senior role and my responsibilities grew, that I saw how flawed my "always-on" approach had become.

Simply put, I observed many successful leaders doing the exact opposite of what I was doing—creating clear boundaries around their time and space. My boat was taking on water at every turn, while theirs seemed to float effortlessly across the calm surface.

What was I doing wrong?

My manager was direct with her feedback: "You need to change how you manage your time, so that you can focus on high priorities first. You aren't delivering on what's expected; what I'm seeing is a lot of busywork but few tangible outcomes."

She was right. I struggled to move projects forward because I was trying to do it all. I would spend hours in my inbox, replying to low-value emails, rather than tackling the more challenging, but more important, tasks.

Over the years—through my career and the executives, authors, and thought leaders I speak to on *The New Leader* podcast—I've picked up several valuable lessons about how successful people manage their time and energy at work.

## Live by your calendar, not your inbox

On my podcast, I make it a point to ask every guest this question, "What's one tool you use to stay on top of things and be productive?" The most common response I've heard? A calendar.

It's arguably the most effective tool to maximize your time because it's finite. It challenges you to be critical in scheduling and acts as an inbox filter for what's truly a priority—you cannot fit every email request into your calendar, so force ranking becomes necessary. Of course, working from your inbox or making long to-do lists can be fun, because of the dopamine hit you get from "checking" another item off the list. But if those items don't translate into practical time in your day, they become extra sources of stress.

As I progressed in my career, I was fortunate enough to observe skilled professionals around me and change my approach. Instead of getting sucked into the email vortex and responding reactively each week, I started to organize my calendar *first*, based on priority. On Sundays, I dedicated 30 minutes to scheduling my upcoming week. I blocked off empty pockets of time on my calendar during which I could do heads-down work and focus my energy on high-priority tasks or key projects (usually between 9 a.m. and 12:30 p.m., two to three days a week).

This approach helped me in two ways:

- I felt much more confident and in control of my week, as I knew where I had to focus.

- My output started to improve. Instead of just working through my emails and responding to urgencies, I was doing what I was hired to do—deliver results.

You can do the same by creating calendar pockets that align to your optimal state or the times of day when you feel most focused and energized.

➤ **PRO TIP: Find your ultradian rhythm.**

Most of us are familiar with the concept of circadian rhythm, but there is also a lesser-known concept called *ultradian rhythm* that plays a key role in determining our energy levels.

In the 1960s, sleep researcher Nathaniel Kleitman discovered what he called the "basic rest-activity cycle"—90-minute periods at night in which we move through various sleep patterns (from light to deep, and so on). He also observed the same 90-minute periods occurring during the day, when we move between higher and lower levels of alertness. He called this pattern the ultradian rhythm.

To find your ultradian rhythm, ask yourself, "When do I have the most energy and focus during the day? When do I start to fade and hit a wall?" Your calendar pockets should reflect the cycles when your mind is most fertile. For me, that was from 9:00 a.m. to 10:30 a.m. and 11:00 a.m. to 12:30 p.m., with a 30-minute break in between. If my day went sideways in the afternoon, I experienced less stress knowing I had been effective when it mattered.

As a young professional, employing this approach can demonstrate to senior leaders that you are capable, efficient, and honing an important skill for future roles.

## Think in waves

If leveraging our calendars is a micro strategy, thinking in waves can be considered a macro one. I recently interviewed author, professor, and HBR contributor Dorie Clark about her new book, *Playing the Long Game: How to Be a Long-Term Thinker in a Short-Term World.* She revealed the notion of "thinking in waves," an approach for making smart choices about where to allocate your time.

The essence is that you cannot accomplish everything right now, so instead begin thinking longer term and approach your time in six- to 12-month phases. Clark told me, "This approach enables me to focus when needed, cluster similar tasks (to lessen the cognitive load of multitasking), and stay refreshed by changing my routines."

Basically, the advice here is to take the long view. Look at the goals you need to accomplish over the next year, prioritize what is most important, and cut or reschedule the ones that can be moved back to avoid overwhelming yourself.

For example, let's say you are a product manager with a launch date scheduled for six months from now. That project will likely constitute a reasonable wave of committed, heads-down work. Where you can veer off track is trying to deliver on that product launch while also trying to join a committee, learn a new instrument, and train for an intensive athletic endeavor. You may end up spreading yourself too thin instead of focusing on your main priority.

All things can be done well, but not *all at once*.

▶ **PRO TIP: Distinguish "heads-up" work from "heads-down" work.**

The whole concept of thinking in waves originates from a concept called "heads up, heads down" first articulated by Jared Kleinert. As professionals working in a fast-paced world, we can easily get distracted or pulled off course. Knowing when to be in heads-up mode vs. heads-down mode, "enables you to leverage the power of focus to your advantage," Clark said.

For instance, perhaps you are new to an industry or organization. Begin by focusing on the important heads-down work to get a feel for your role. Your first six months can be a learning wave (studying your field, building new skills), followed by a creation wave (sharing your insights within the company, publishing content on LinkedIn).

After a year of heads-down work, it's now time to shift into heads-up mode. For the next 12 months, you can focus on building your network by attending conferences, webinars, or speaking at workshops. Looking back over this two-year period, you have now built some solid career pillars while others are still worrying about what to do next.

The key here is to avoid short-term thinking and play the long game.

## Don't fight the truth of time

No matter how hard we try, there are only 24 hours in a day. Overplanning creates an ecosystem in which we are constantly moving from task to task and draining ourselves in the process.

Productivity expert Dave Crenshaw, who had the most popular LinkedIn Learning course of 2020, put it this way, "It has been taught that happiness comes from spending one dollar less than what you have, and misery comes from spending one dollar more than what you have. When you overspend with money, you go into debt and have to pay interest. It is the same with time."

I'd never considered the concept of time bankruptcy before reading Dave's work. It gave me pause. I began embracing the concept of *underspending time*, viewing it as a positive marker to my overall health and well-being. When I shifted my mindset in this way, I was less riddled with guilt when stepping outside for fresh air or refilling my water bottle while doing a few stretches between virtual meetings. Before, I was playing a constant game of catch-up ("I can never find the time!").

Dave summarizes it well: "Be at peace with the truth of time. Learn to accept it as the immovable truth that it is. It allows you to feel time-wealthy and smoothly manage unexpected emergencies."

➤ **PRO TIP: Start small.**

While it may be impossible to ditch a back-to-back meeting schedule overnight, there are things you can do.

A great starting point is to build buffers into your schedule to avoid overplanning. Start small, inserting 15-minute blocks into your day that act as protected time. Carving out these small moments creates space to catch your breath.

Another approach is to protect your time fiercely. At work, we often get roped into ad hoc conversations or projects because they sound fun or interesting in the moment (or because we struggle with saying no). But the reality is that no one is going to protect your time for you. That's your responsibility.

The next time you find yourself facing an ask that encroaches on your time, try responding with, "I have a timeline I am working on right now—can we speak later?" Odds are, that person may seek out someone else if it's urgent, absolving you from yet another distraction. If it's truly you that they need, you can arrange to connect when it best suits you. By setting boundaries, you indicate to the other person that you are willing to engage but know how to prioritize like a pro.

Keep in mind that time management isn't a one-time activity. You'll have to adjust your approach and see what works for you over time. The above strategies are a great way to start. Give yourself permission to use them—your work (and your life) will be better for it.

### QUICK RECAP

We often think that staying on top of the requests we receive, instantly responding to them, and saying yes to everything is a marker of success. But this can prove harmful. There are ways to create clear boundaries around your time and space.

- Live by your calendar, not your inbox.

- Look at your long-term goals and prioritize what's most important.

- Build buffers into your schedule to avoid overplanning.

Adapted from "3 Practical Ways to Be More Productive" on hbr.org, November 12, 2021 (product #H06P4F).

Watch this video to learn about promising productivity methods:

# 14

# Are You Taking On Too Many Nonpromotable Tasks?

by Linda R. Babcock, Brenda Peyser, Lise Vesterlund, and Laurie Weingart

Luna, a sixth-year associate at a prestigious law firm (and a young woman we know), loved her job. When her boss asked her to help run the summer intern program, she immediately said yes. It was a chance for her to learn about different departments, meet partners, and showcase her organizational skills. She put a lot of time and energy into it. But once performance reviews rolled around, her efforts were never mentioned. Instead, her boss warned Luna that her billable hours had fallen behind. She was baffled and disappointed—what she thought would benefit her career didn't seem to matter at all.

Does this situation sound familiar? We're not surprised.

Like Luna, many workers we've encountered during the research for our book, *The No Club: Putting a Stop to Women's*

*Dead-End Work*, devote excessive hours to tasks that help their organizations but do nothing to advance their careers. These are known as *nonpromotable tasks (NPTs)* or unrewarded responsibilities. Maybe you're the person who trains new hires, takes notes at a meeting, organizes the holiday party, fills in for absent colleagues, or handles that low-revenue and time-consuming client. Everyone benefits when these NPTs get done. But sadly, and too often, the person who does them ends up robbed of valuable time and the promotable work that actually grows paychecks and careers.

Our research shows that this problem is particularly pernicious for women.[1] We asked the management team at a professional services firm to rank work assignments by how promotable they were, and then examined how employees spent their time. We found that, independent of rank, the median female employee spent 200 more hours per year on nonpromotable work than her male counterparts. To put that into perspective: Women spent an additional month on dead-end assignments.

Further, in a controlled setting where men and women were equally good at executing NPTs, we found that women were handling a greater number of them—not due to preference or attitude—but because they were *expected* to say yes more often.[2] As a result, women were asked and volunteered to do NPTs frequently, while men got a free pass.

This is why, especially for women, understanding what assignments are nonpromotable, the consequences of taking them on, and the reasons you might feel pressure to say yes can help you steer clear of Luna's mistake.

# How to Identify Nonpromotable Tasks

Nonpromotable tasks have several recognizable characteristics.

## NPTs are not instrumental to your organization's mission

All organizations have goals and objectives, and they value some more than others. The less a task aligns with those objectives, the lower its promotability. For Luna, serving clients is her organization's mission, meaning anything that takes time away from that, like administering the summer intern program, is likely to be nonpromotable. Luna's performance evaluation was less stellar than she wanted because she spent too much time on a task that wasn't directly connected to the bottom line.

## NPTs are often not visible to others

Less-visible tasks tend to be nonpromotable because other people cannot see your efforts or impact. NPTs are often done in support of the team's work in a way that can't be credited to you—like editing your coworker's section of the report or making the team's presentations "look pretty." Only Luna's boss knew about her work on the summer intern program. It was invisible to everyone else.

NPTs may not require specialized skills,
and many people can do them

Promotable tasks leverage the unique skills you were hired for; NPTs do not. Gathering résumés, scheduling appointments, and compiling interviewers' notes are tasks Luna took on that almost anyone in the firm could have performed. None of these tasks relied on her legal knowledge or abilities.

## Why We Feel Pressured to Say Yes

There are several reasons why we sometimes feel pressured to say yes, even when we don't have to. Here are some patterns we observed in our research.

### You think you need to decide immediately

We often feel the urgency of a request, even more so if it comes from someone more powerful or higher up in the organization than ourselves. For instance, let's say you bump into your boss in the hallway, and they ask you to take on a task. You may think you need to respond then and there—but you don't.

Rather than automatically saying yes, buy time to gather information, evaluate the task, and think about your career objectives and what you need to do to get there. Here's a rule we use for ourselves: Wait at least 24 hours before saying yes. Instead of "Sure," tell the requester: "Thanks so much for thinking of me for this. I need some time to think about it and how it fits in with my other priorities. I'll be sure to get back to you by end of day tomorrow." That will make it easier to say no later.

## You have internalized the expectation that you should say yes

Recognize that your discomfort and reluctance to say no (when you are asked once again to "take one for the team") likely stems from you internalizing the expectations others have of you. This is especially true for women, who may say yes to an NPT to avoid feeling guilty about failing to live up to these expectations.

The next time you are asked to volunteer, ask yourself if doing this task is the best use of your time. If the answer is no, then sit back and let someone else come forward, or better yet, propose that the task be randomly assigned, or that everyone takes turns doing the work.

## You are flattered to be asked

When you feel honored to have been asked, it's hard to see the downside. Luna said yes because she felt good that her boss had noticed her abilities.

While it's nice to be called on, that positive feeling will quickly disappear once you become buried in the actual work. And if the task is mostly invisible—like organizing an internship program was—it will provide no tangible upside. Remember, you can still feel flattered that you were asked, even if you are able to decline.

# How to Weigh an Opportunity

The next time you're asked to do an NPT, give yourself some time and use it to carefully evaluate the consequences of taking on the work. Be cognizant of the mistakes you might make when deciding whether to say yes or no.

## Consider the "implicit no" of saying yes

When you take on a new NPT, you will have less time to do something else. When you agree to help another team streamline their workflow, you are implicitly saying no to another activity you could do in that time. It may be time spent helping your team with a new product launch where the opportunity cost of helping someone else do their job can be high. Luna's implicit no was her billable work. By adding the intern program, she had to cut back on her client hours, which hurt her performance review.

## Weigh the urgency of the task

A task with a short deadline will trump a task with a longer one, no matter how insignificant it is. The big tasks, such as recruiting new clients, may not be very time sensitive, so taking on an NPT or two with short time horizons is likely to put off longer-term initiatives that are more valued by your organization.

## Remember that you will also be busy in the future

Your calendar looks clear three months out, so today's "yes" doesn't seem so bad. But chances are that your current rush of activity will be the same three months from now. Before you say yes, imagine instead that this distant request is for next week. Would you be as excited to plan the office party next week with your current workload? Probably not!

## Evaluate the indirect benefits of the NPT

Not all NPTs are the same. Be intentional in choosing NPTs that are best for you. Some nonpromotable tasks can help you later. We call these tasks *indirectly promotable*—they might help you gain knowledge, develop skills, or connections that you can leverage later on. Other NPTs are attractive because they align with your personal mission, like advancing diversity, equity, and inclusion initiatives. In addition to considering the cost of taking on the NPT, be sure to assess the potential benefits. Knowing that most of us will have to do an NPT from time to time, try to choose the ones that are best for you.

. . .

Your road to success will be shorter if you recognize and steer toward the assignments that matter most for your career. You'll be surprised by the recognition you'll receive when you finally have the time for the work that is valued most by your organization.

## QUICK RECAP

Though nonpromotable tasks (NPTs) are often crucial to an organization's success, they rarely contribute to an employee's career progression. Next time you're asked to do an NPT, give yourself some time to carefully evaluate the consequences of taking on the work.

- Consider the "implicit no" of saying yes.

- Weigh the urgency of the task.

- Evaluate the indirect benefits of the NPT.

Adapted from "Are You Taking On Too Many Non-Promotable Tasks?" on hbr.org, April 26, 2022 (product #H0701E).

# 15

# How to Stop Scrolling and Focus at Work

by Amantha Imber

When I go upstairs to start work for the day in my home office, there is one big predictor of how productive I'm going to be—whether my mobile phone comes with me or whether I deliberately (or accidentally) leave it downstairs.

Sadly, this morning, my phone was by my side. As I wrote this piece, every time I felt stuck, I unconsciously picked it up and scrolled through social media for relief. The new messages, likes, and followers instantly made me feel better. But they also made me reluctant to go back to work, because Microsoft Word failed to fill me with the same positive reinforcement.

"If I find it difficult to not be distracted by my phone, how about younger professionals who are a mobile-first generation?" I thought.

Being the first generation to be raised entirely on tech, as a Gen Zer, you likely spend half your waking hours scrolling through your phones. You're also more likely than millennials to be hooked to your phones—research shows that 31% of Gen Zers feel uncomfortable if they are without their phone for 30 minutes or less, 58% check their emails multiple times a day, and over a quarter use their phones for 10 or more hours.[1] While we have become potentially more reliant on devices and technologies than any other generation, we cannot let them undermine our ability to focus and work smart.

I spoke with various guests on my podcast to learn how they keep distractions at bay and get work done. Here are a few tactics we discussed to help you stay focused when you need to get things done.

## Use a struggle timer

I recently chatted with Scott Young, the critically acclaimed author of *Ultralearning*, about how to get better at staying focused on a task.[2] Young believes that our ability to concentrate depends on how well we can manage our emotions. Making progress on big, important projects is often frustrating, involves getting negative feedback, and at times, questioning our abilities. These challenges can create an instinctual aversion to maintaining focus. This morning, for example, writer's block frustrated me and, instead of staying in the flow, I reached for my phone.

Young has tried several strategies to improve his capacity to stay focused and reduce digital distractions. One of them is called the "struggle timer." The idea emerged when he was contemplating his approach to studying and learning new material. One of his many accomplishments is that he learned the entire MIT computer science curriculum—which normally takes four years—in less than 12 months. And he did this without taking any classes.

When Young was working on solving a problem during the course, he would often wonder: How quickly should he look at the answer when he couldn't identify the right one? "The approach that I took during the MIT challenge was, as soon as I got stuck, I looked at the right answer, because immediate feedback is important to learning," he told me. But that also broke his flow.

Over the years, Young shifted his view. He now believes it often makes sense to struggle a little bit on harder problems for two reasons. First, you can sometimes solve the problem with a bit more time, so struggling for a little longer can be even more beneficial to your learning and forces you to stay in the flow. Second, Young believes that sitting in the struggle allows you to appreciate the right answer more once you do find it. The solution will be much more memorable when you go through and overcome your initial frustration, he explained. It's the difference between actually figuring out how to solve a problem and looking up the answer, then thinking, "Oh, that makes sense."

Young took these insights and now, when he feels himself struggling with a problem or a task, he sets the struggle timer for five or 10 minutes. Often, this additional time helps him stay in the flow instead of giving up or procrastinating.

## Create stuck scripts

A professor of marketing at New York University's Stern School of Business, Adam Alter experiences stuck points frequently. But instead of automatically reaching for his phone to relieve his unpleasant emotions, he does something else. "The best thing you can do is to have a script that you follow in those moments, especially if you regularly hit these points where your default would be to check the phone," Alter told me.

For example, every time you hit a stuck point, Alter suggests telling yourself that you'll go for a two-minute walk. "I often do this. I walk around the floor in my office building. And at home, I'll just take a stroll outside or I'll walk upstairs from my office, which is in the basement."

This short walk is a natural way for him to reset. After walking, he sits back down and finds it easier to pick his work back up.

Another strategy Alter uses is switching tasks. Instead of getting distracted and squandering time, he'll reach for a simpler task when he feels stuck on something difficult. "Whenever I hit the wall on the primary stuff, such as writing a paper, I turn to the secondary stuff, so it's time spent wisely," he explains. For instance, as a researcher, Alter tries to stay up to date with the newest findings in his field. He's frequently sent the tables of contents for academic journals, but rarely has time to go through them properly. When he feels stuck on a task, however, he's learned that he can shift his mindset by reading through these journals rather than giving up altogether.

## Leave your phone behind

Phones are, well, one of the biggest distractions when it comes to getting work done. Research has shown that the average person touches their phone 2,617 times per day.[3] That's a lot of swiping, typing, scrolling, and clicking—and much of this occurs when we're procrastinating on the task at hand or are experiencing negative emotions around the task (frustration, boredom, etc.).

We often say to ourselves, "I need to check my phone less." But this strategy relies on pure willpower, and sadly, willpower is a limited resource. Perhaps it's time for a more extreme strategy that physically restricts us from using our phones.

Prior to becoming the CEO of Moment, a company that helps people use their phones in healthier ways, Tim Kendall was the president of Pinterest. During this time, he struggled a lot with his phone usage. He started to research what he describes as "brute force approaches" and discovered a product called the kSafe.

The kSafe is a lockable kitchen safe with a built-in timer. It was originally designed as a weight-loss aid in which dieters could lock away unhealthy food, but in recent years, the product has found a secondary purpose for those struggling with mobile phone addiction, as it's the perfect size to lock away smartphones.

Kendall initially tried experimenting with locking away his phone on weeknights and then for a few hours on the weekend. While he doesn't use the kSafe regularly anymore, he found it effective at the time.

"The thing that works for me today is, I have an office in my house, and when I leave that office to go and have dinner with my family, I just leave my phone in the office," he said. "On my best nights, I don't go and get my phone until the next morning, which is effectively the same thing as putting it in a kitchen safe from 6 p.m. to 8 a.m."

I'm not asking you to go buy a kSafe, but one way to maintain your focus is to leave your phone in the furthest spot possible when you're beginning a task. If you're working in a huddle room in your office, for instance, leave your phone in your desk drawer. When you hit a stuck point, you'll be less motivated to walk all the way across the hall just to check your Instagram.

· · ·

We all lose focus from time to time, but staying focused is imperative if you want to be productive. Focus helps us get into a rhythm, be consistent, and produce better results. The thing is, our minds are powerful, and we can train our minds to ignore distractions. Use these tips to make small changes and use your time in meaningful ways.

## QUICK RECAP

It's easy to be distracted when we're working, especially by our phones. It's imperative to reduce digital distractions and get work done.

- Use a struggle timer. If you find yourself stuck on a problem, set your struggle timer for five or 10 minutes to work it out and stay in the flow.

- Create and follow stuck scripts, which could be as simple as, "When I have a writer's block, I'll take a two-minute walk."

- Leave your phone in the most inaccessible spot possible when you're beginning a task.

---

Adapted from content posted on hbr.org,
February 22, 2023 (product #H07I1P).

# Take Care of Your Mental and Physical Health

# 16

# A Guide to Managing Your Mental Health

by Ascend Editors

Many of us are feeling anxious and depressed right now. The economy is dwindling. We're hearing more and more about lay-offs. Wars continue to ravage lives. And the health of our planet doesn't seem to be improving.

The unfortunate reality is that it's not a particularly great time in history—and we're all feeling it, especially the younger generations. Globally, more than 20% of people are struggling with anxiety and depression.[1] Forty-eight percent of Gen Zers and 44% of millennials report feeling anxious or stressed all the time.[2]

From our own experiences, we also know that feelings of anxiety and depression can just as easily trickle into our work lives. Sometimes, work can become a trigger and exacerbate our mental health struggles. Because these emotions are so personal and complex, it can feel uncomfortable or isolating to talk about them at work, especially when we're just starting out in our careers. In an international study, 82% of respondents said that they did not feel comfortable talking about mental health at work.[3] In yet another report, 92% of Indian employees said they would prefer talking about their mental health with a robot over a manager.[4]

However, addressing our collective mental health issues at work doesn't need to be taboo. Research tells us that we're likely to be less stressed, happier, and more productive in our jobs when we have more open conversations about mental health.[5]

To address mental health at work, we must become more aware of the stigma around it in this setting, as well as how mental health issues show up for each of us. We have to commit to creating change both at the personal and the leadership level.

## Why Is Mental Health Still Taboo?

A lot of the stigma around mental health—at work and in our lives—is born from a collective misunderstanding about what it means to struggle with emotional well-being. Negative perceptions or patterns of thinking about mental health can show up for several reasons: the way we feel and process our own feelings, how we've been taught and conditioned to think about emotions, how we see others react to these conversations, and finally, what the media (and society at large) tell us about taking care of ourselves.

We still live in a world that creates a false binary between "positive" and "negative" or "good" and "bad" emotions. We still live in a culture that values toxic positivity. Though these ideas are largely systemic, many of us have internalized them. When this happens, the stigma holds strong, and it impacts our ability to make sense of our difficult emotions.

In reality, our emotional health is not so black-and-white.

Susan David, a Harvard Medical School psychologist and author of *Emotional Agility*, states that every emotion we feel is "normal." There is no such thing as a bad emotion.

According to David, the difficult emotions we feel are clues to what matters most to us. To escape the stigma, we need to actively engage with the discomfort that we sometimes feel in life. David adds, "We don't get to have a meaningful career, raise a family, leave the world a better place, or make our way through a pandemic without stress and discomfort. Discomfort is the price of admission to a meaningful life."

To manage (and honor) difficult emotions, David suggests two strategies:

- *Permit yourself to experience the emotion.* Recognize what you're feeling, practice "gentle acceptance" to acknowledge that it's happening, and then respond to that emotion with an open attitude. Let go of what you can't control.

- *Extend compassion to yourself and to others.* Be patient as you try to understand the full reality of your situation. Practice this mantra: Be kind, loving, and courageous.

## How Do We Empower Ourselves to Address Mental Health Better at Work?

### Educate yourself about mental health issues

How often have you used "anxiety" and "stress" interchangeably? Even though anxiety and stress sometimes feel similar, in her article "Am I Anxious or Just Stressed?" author Charlotte Lieberman explains that they are, in fact, different emotional states.

Stress, for instance, is typically defined as a response to an external trigger and can either be acute (a tight deadline) or chronic (persistent financial trouble). Anxiety, on the other hand, is often triggered internally by excessive thoughts—judgments about the past, worries about the future, and so on. When left unchecked, both stress and anxiety can escalate into more severe mental health conditions, or what we call *disorders*.

Why does this difference matter?

Lieberman writes, "While understanding where stress and anxiety come from, and the difference between them won't make your feelings go away, it's the first and most important step to finding freedom from the discomfort—whether on your own or with a therapist."

Moreover, learning to identify how emotions show up, and using the appropriate language to label them, can help us become better at addressing mental health with our peers, colleagues, and friends. With the right tools, we can be more intentional about how we alleviate some of these feelings.

## Be intentional about self-care

First, understand that everyone's needs are different. In her article "There's No 'Right' Way to Do Self-Care," Alyssa F. Westring writes that "figuring out what you need starts by simply noticing what makes you feel good and what makes you drained."

When you do that, it becomes clear that self-care doesn't equate to overhauling your entire life. Instead, Westring says that self-care is about exploring "small, everyday changes that work in the context of your whole life."

Think of some of the habits you practice as part of your everyday life. What's working for you, and what do you feel comfortable leaving behind? Are there any habits you're not currently practicing that you'd like to start?

## Talk to your boss if that feels safe

While there's a lot you can do to manage your emotions, systemic change requires that we break the silence around mental health conversations. According to author Deborah Grayson Riegel, this often starts by acknowledging our own struggles and sharing them with our managers and leaders. That said, this may not always be safe or feasible—especially if your workplace is not psychologically safe or inclusive.

In her article "Should You Talk to Your Boss About Your Mental Health?" Riegel cautions against disclosing your mental health conditions under pressure. She writes, "Never pressure yourself to disclose if you're not ready. If you feel that you have more to lose than to gain, or need more time to come to a decision, don't force it (and be patient with yourself along the way)."

If you do feel confident having this conversation with your manager, there are a lot of potential positives to opening up. But do so strategically.

## If you're a new (or seasoned) manager, advocate for your team

When people in positions of power speak up about their mental health struggles, it makes it safer for their employees and teams to open up as well. If you're a new manager or emerging leader, you have the power to impact your work culture in a positive way.

In the article "New Managers, You Can Create a Workplace That Values Mental Health," author Craig Cowdrey recommends that first-time managers take on five different roles to become an agent of change and advocate for workplaces that value mental health.

- *The embracer:* Change is not going to be comfortable at first and will require a deliberate, conscious effort on your part. Start by unlearning your own biases and assumptions about other people and their needs at work.

- *The investigator:* Spend time understanding your company's policies. Read up on the latest global research on best practices for employee well-being and engagement. In addition, conduct your own anonymous surveys and one-on-one feedback sessions to understand what you can do better day-to-day.

- *The challenger:* Critically assess and identify outdated processes, practices, or systems that no longer work for your team, such as inflexible working hours, poor leave policies, or lack of psychologically safe spaces.

- *The integrator:* Create a transparent chain of communication between the different stakeholders—your team,

HR, and leadership. You're in a unique position to have access to all of them.

- *The advocator:* Sure, you must speak up for your team. But more importantly, speak up about your own experiences. When you open up in this way, you help everyone—senior leaders, peers, and direct reports—see your "humanness."

## QUICK RECAP

Feelings of anxiety and depression can easily trickle into our work lives. We all need to get better at addressing mental health at work.

- Change needs to happen at both personal and leadership levels. This starts by understanding why mental health stigma exists.

- To escape the stigma, we need to actively engage with the discomfort that we sometimes feel around mental health issues.

- Become more intentional about addressing emotions by managing your emotional health or advocating for your team's well-being and promoting a more inclusive workplace.

Adapted from content posted on hbr.org, October 6, 2022 (product #H079LE).

In this video, Christine Liu interviews Susan David about how to manage difficult emotions—in life and at work:

# There's No "Right" Way to Do Self-Care

by Alyssa F. Westring

There's no shortage of advice touting the importance of self-care. We're being told to meditate, take long baths, and purchase new and expensive products. Though this advice is well-intentioned, it rarely gets to the heart of why so many of us struggle to nurture our mental and physical health.

As a researcher, teacher, and career coach, I've been studying this issue for nearly two decades. On a daily basis, I hear from people who *want* to take better care of themselves but can't seem to find the time. It always falls to the bottom of their to-do lists—after they fulfill their responsibilities to their bosses, colleagues, families, and friends.

Finding time for self-care can be especially difficult for students and young professionals. The pressing urge to prioritize school, work, and job applications is overwhelming. Not surprisingly, by the end of the day, many people are left drained and have little motivation to focus on themselves.

The irony here is that making the time for self-care is essential to performing well in all the other areas of our lives. Ample research has shown that nurturing our brains, bodies, and spirits can help us be more effective at whatever we put our minds to.[1] So how do we reconcile this apparent paradox: Our mental and physical health is important for our educations and careers, but our educations and careers impede the time and energy we have for our mental and physical health?

The solution isn't a better study or workout routine or the right sleep or meditation app. To change what we do, we have to change how we think.

In my research with organizational psychologist Stew Friedman, we've found that most people operate with a trade-off mentality (e.g., "If I want to perform better at work, I need to take time away from something else"). This mindset is ingrained in the way we're taught to view the different parts of life from a young age—even the notion of work-life "balance" is frequently represented as a scale with work on one side and the rest of life on the other. And while it's true that there are limits to our time, it is this exact mindset that often stops us from making positive changes.

To create this positive change, we need to reframe how we view the interconnections between the different parts of our lives. By challenging your assumptions about self-care, you can find an approach that works for you.

Here are three tools that can help.

## Define self-care on your own terms

Given the abundance of advice about self-care, most of us are operating with a set of assumptions about what wellness *should* look like. But only you can determine what your mind, body, and spirit need to thrive.

Maybe that's an episode of reality television to unwind at the end of the day. Maybe it's finding a therapist or psychiatrist to support you. Or maybe you're someone who needs to mute a text chain or Reddit thread that is causing you angst.

To figure out what you need, start by simply noticing when you feel invigorated and when you feel drained. Look for patterns. What makes you feel good? What makes you feel overwhelmed and anxious? Now begin creating your own understanding of what self-care looks like to you.

## Check for all-or-nothing thinking

Notice how you think about making time for yourself. Do you assume that you need to completely overhaul your lifestyle? You might be surprised at the number of people I work with who think that they need to go from sleep-deprived and burned out to a health and fitness guru overnight. The idea of doing anything less than a total life transformation is unacceptable, so they avoid making any changes at all. This isn't surprising given all the marketing that promises a "new you," but it definitely isn't helpful.

Noticing whether you're engaging in all-or-nothing thinking is the first step to creating a more realistic mentality. From there, you can start to explore small, doable changes that work in the context of your whole life. As you learn what works and what doesn't, curiosity and self-compassion are great alternatives to all-or-nothing thinking and tend to yield longer-lasting change.

## Seek opportunities to integrate

Another mindset shift is challenging the assumption that prioritizing wellness is something that we must do separately from the other parts of our lives. My research has shown that the most sustainable self-care solutions frequently come from bringing the different parts of our lives together.

For example, consider how self-care time could also be used to enrich your career (planning a walking meeting with a colleague or mentor instead of a Zoom call), support your community (picking up trash around the neighborhood), or strengthen other relationships in your life (setting a recurring time to stream yoga videos with a long-distance friend or family member).

. . .

By changing the way you think about self-care, you can make incremental and meaningful shifts that bring you greater peace, energy, and joy. In doing so, you can experience for yourself what research has clearly shown—that investments in your well-being can actually enhance your professional success.[2] It is possible to create harmony among the different parts of your life, but you might have to challenge some of your assumptions to do so.

## QUICK RECAP

Finding time to take care of your mind and body can feel impossible. But the answer isn't a better workout routine or sleep app—it's changing your mindset. By challenging your assumptions about self-care, you can find an approach that works for you.

- Self-care can look different for different people. Only you can determine what your mind, body, and spirit need to thrive.

- To figure out what you need, start by simply noticing when you feel invigorated and when you feel drained.

- Look out for all-or-nothing thinking, as it can cause you to put too much pressure on yourself and avoid making any changes at all.

- Explore small, doable changes that work in the context of your whole life.

---

Adapted from content posted on hbr.org,
April 20, 2021 (product #H06B2B).

# 18

# You Don't Have to Be the Best at Everything

by Morra Aarons-Mele

A few years ago, I was in a therapy session, talking about how anxious I felt about bombing an important presentation at work. My therapist turned to me and said, "Why do you have to be so special at everything? Whoever told you that?" I looked at her and said, "I've always been special, since I was three years old." To which my therapist replied, "Well, who says?"

It's a question I've pondered many times since, and one I ask myself when my inner critic takes charge. I'm an anxious achiever, ambitious and career focused. My anxiety prompts me to overperform. I can never rest until I've reached the next goal and done it to perfection. Thoughts of failure have driven me to accomplish many things, but the anxiety driving those fears takes a toll on my mental health, my relationships, and my ability to experience joy.

Who said I have to be so special? Who said I have to be great all the time? If you also struggle with perfectionism, driven by anxiety, this question can be profound.

Many anxious achievers push themselves to the point of over-work in an effort to achieve impossible standards. We often act this way out of habit. Somewhere along the way—through messages we received in our childhoods, our adolescence, or even in our educations and early careers—we internalized the thinking that if we make mistakes, we're not worthy. Now, these internal voices threaten, shame, and harshly critique us in life and at work. Anxiety has become the driver that powers us through.

The problem is that anxiety is not a sustainable motivator and perfectionism often causes procrastination. When the stakes of failing feel too high, we're more likely to avoid rather than do. Once a task is done, we may look back and be unable to find anything positive in our performance. We measure our self-worth by our self-imposed standards, and the cycle continues. Inevitably, we become burned out.

So, how do we overcome the cycle?

## Understanding Your Inner Critic

I recently interviewed Google's Newton Cheng for my podcast. Our conversation gave us both more insight into our anxious achiever tendencies. Like me (and maybe you, too), Newton pushes himself to do great things as a way of working through anxiety. Also like many of us, Newton deals with an inner critic. I call it "the voice."

On our journeys to perfectionism, "the voice" often targets the piece of us that always expects to be the best and asks: "How dare you be less than perfect?" Newton's voice tells him, "You're lazy . . . You're lazy . . . You're lazy." Although, of course, he's the opposite of lazy. Newton is a successful professional, working as an executive at one of the world's most admired companies. He's also a world-champion powerlifter who holds records at the global, national, and state level for his age and weight class.

After a lot of internal work and therapy, Newton told me he's started to pay attention to his patterns of thinking. He tries to recognize when that voice inside his head is a saboteur driven by anxiety as opposed to a champion driven by his value of showing up as best as he can. That's the first step to turning the volume down.

What does the saboteur in your head sound like? Maybe it says, "If you work hard enough, you can't fail. So, work harder." Maybe, like Newton's voice, it says, "You're lazy. Do better. People are depending on you." Or maybe it tells you that your best is never good enough.

Whatever message the voice is sending, pay attention to it. When you feel yourself becoming discouraged by your own thoughts, it's important to slow down, and acknowledge that "the voice" is not *your voice*—it's your anxiety and it doesn't tell the truth. This isn't easy to do. Most of us anxious achievers have become so accustomed to listening to our inner critic that we do it out of habit. We don't know any other way to operate. But with practice and self-awareness, we can learn how to manage.

Here are three steps you can do to quiet "the voice" down:

## 1. Notice when "the voice" strikes

The next time you hear a critique in your head, consider the following:

- Notice who is speaking. Does the voice sound like you, or does it sound like someone from your past? Sometimes our inner critics are driven by formative experiences or by people we encountered years before.

- What phrases does the voice use? Notice the words your inner critic tends to say over and over. Is the voice a harsh taskmaster who shows up when you make a mistake? Or is it a nagging little bug constantly buzzing in your ear? Paying attention to these cues will help you identify when it's speaking.

- How do you feel right before the voice takes over? What emotions tend to precede it? For example, you might notice that you feel anxious right before your inner critic tells you to pull an all-nighter on a presentation. What's making you anxious? What could help calm the anxiety in that moment?

- Does listening to the voice serve you? For example, is your voice driving you to be people-pleasing? Have you caught yourself bending over backward to help someone who really didn't need the help? Perhaps your inner critic is demanding that you make everyone happy, at your own expense. Next time the voice tells you to clean up the conference table after a lunch meeting, acknowledge it—and then tell it to be quiet.

## 2. Address "the voice" with compassion

Only after you notice the themes and commonalities in your favorite self-criticisms can you attempt to address them head-on.

An easy way to start: Address the voice in the third person, out loud. Here's where practicing self-compassion comes in, and it's a wonderful skill to learn.

Self-compassion means being deliberately kind to yourself instead of fighting your anxiety or relying on self-criticism to motivate you. In practice, it looks like addressing the voice with understanding and generosity. Sometimes I call this approach the "sweetheart method." (My therapist told me it would help if I called myself "sweetheart" when addressing the voice.) So, now, when I notice my anxiety trying to scare me into perfectionism, I'll say aloud to myself, "Now, sweetheart, you're not lazy because you decided not to write that blog post. You're being strategic. Your time is valuable, and you don't need to work for free when you're busy being paid for other work."

Honestly, it helps. You don't have to call yourself sweetheart—pick any word that's right for you!

## 3. Use an exercise to summon deliberate kindness

Here is an exercise I've adapted from Dr. Kristin Neff, an expert on self-compassion. She suggests, "Instead of self-judgment, show yourself self-kindness." Here's how it works.

- Simply sit and place your hands on your chest. Feel your breath, in and out.

- Connect with the feeling of your hands on your sternum. Take a moment of stillness.

- Think of something you did well recently. It could be something you rocked at work or the fact that you fit a workout into a busy day. It could be a kind text message you sent to a friend—anything you did that made you feel good.

- Hold your chest, think through that moment, and tell yourself, "I did a good job." Try to really feel it.

- When you're done, don't jump to a negative self-criticism or the next item on your to-do list. Just sit with the feeling of self-compassion for a moment.

When we take moments to reward ourselves for the small things, we learn to be kinder to ourselves, quiet those inner critics, and interrupt self-sabotaging habits.

. . .

The psychologist David Burns says that giving up on always being special means we are just human after all. Anxious achievers, perhaps even more than most people, need to look our ego in the eye and realize: We don't have to be perfect, and we don't have to be better than others. We have the right to fail and carry on anyway. We have the right to have a crummy day or miss a deadline every now and then. "When you no longer need to be special," Burns' colleague Taylor Chesney, PsyD, once said, "life becomes special."

Can you picture a life in which you achieve at the same high levels you do now, but without all the anxiety, stress, and self-criticism that comes from listening to the voice? Can you imagine a world in which you manage your angst, instead of it controlling you? Maybe you could put it to work and channel the motivation it can bring. You don't have to give up your identity as an anxious achiever—but you can have more power over your feelings and how you respond to them.

Without all the negative outcomes that come from holding yourself to a standard that's literally impossible to reach, you might just unlock your creativity and let loose your drive—and your joy—in an entirely new way. Next time you hear "the voice," listen for the clues that will help you diffuse it in the future. Find a way to be kind to yourself, and ask yourself the question: Why do I have to be so special?

## QUICK RECAP

Many anxious achievers push themselves to the point of overwork in an effort to achieve impossible standards. Our internal voices threaten, shame, and critique us in life and at work. Anxiety has become the driver that powers us through. But anxiety is not a sustainable motivator, and perfectionism often causes procrastination.

- Sometimes, our inner critics are driven by formative experiences or by people we encountered years before.

- Address your inner critic with compassion. Be deliberately kind to yourself.

- Engage in a moment of kindness by thinking of something you did well recently and telling yourself you did a good job.

Adapted from content posted on hbr.org, May 8, 2023.

# 19

# To Improve Your Work Performance, Get Some Exercise

by Bonnie Hayden Cheng and Yolanda Na Li

Worldwide, 1.4 billion adults are insufficiently active, with one in three women and one in four men not engaging in adequate physical activity.[1] In fact, there has been no improvement in physical activity levels since 2001, and physical inactivity is twice as prevalent in high-income countries than in low-income countries.

To combat the negative impact of physical inactivity, the World Health Organization (WHO) launched a global action plan in 2018 aimed at reducing physical inactivity by 15% by 2030. By promoting physical activity and encouraging individuals to engage in regular exercise, the WHO seeks to maximize the benefits of physical activity: preventing and managing noncommunicable diseases like cardiovascular diseases (including coronary heart disease and stroke), various types of cancer, improving overall physical and mental well-being, sharpening cognitive capacity, and ensuring healthy growth and development.

Although the beneficial effects of physical activity on general well-being are widely acknowledged, there has been a lack of research on how it impacts outcomes at work, including job performance and health. This is all the more important as various emerging work modes have allowed for greater flexibility and convenience. Yet we're finding ourselves sitting more and moving less, as many of us no longer have to commute to work or walk from meeting to meeting.

## How Physical Activity Affects Work Performance

Given that most of our waking hours are spent working, in an effort to support the WHO's initiative to increase physical activity, our recent research points to some important work-related implications of physical activity.[2]

Approximately 200 employees from the UK and China participated in a 10-day study in which we captured self-reported and objective physical activity data (via a wearable smart band device), as well as self- and supervisor-reported work outcomes. We uncovered some noteworthy findings about daily physical activity that impact employees and organizations.

### Motivation for physical activity predicts physical activity

It may seem obvious that being *motivated* to partake in an activity would lead to *doing* said activity, but anyone who has ever made and then abandoned a New Year's resolution knows this isn't necessarily the case. People's *autonomous motivation*, a stable individual difference reflecting the degree to which one feels self-determined to engage in a behavior, is a critical personal resource that can prompt individuals to engage in physical activity. Importantly, the more autonomous the form of motivation—in other words, the more people consider physical activity to be a fun and enjoyable activity rather than something to dread—the more likely they are to engage in daily physical activity.

## Physical activity generates next-day, work-relevant resources

We found that daily physical activity engendered a package of next-day resources, called *resource caravans*, that contributed to work-related outcomes.

The first resource immediately afforded by physical activity is quality sleep, or a person's degree of satisfaction with their daily sleep experience. Physical activity promotes protein synthesis and facilitates quality sleep as a homeostatic feedback process benefiting the body and brain. The second resource gain is vigor, an affective resource associated with energy and vitality. The third resource gain is task focus, a cognitive resource that supports enhanced information processing, attention, and concentration.

## Physical activity improves next-day job performance and health

Existing research on the impact of physical activity in the work context has focused on physical activity during specific periods (e.g., exercising over the lunch break), neglecting consideration of physical activity throughout the whole day. This has further contributed to inconsistent findings, as employees may perceive a depletion of resources (such as vigor and concentration) immediately after physical activity, which may actually interfere with their work.

All this is to say that it may take some time to experience the work-related benefits of physical activity. Sure enough, our research finds time-lagged benefits of physical activity on *next-day* task performance, creativity, and health symptoms. Across two studies, we consistently found that employees' daily physical activity throughout the day generates resource caravans consisting of physical (sleep), affective (vigor), and cognitive (task focus) resources, which further contribute to next-day job performance and health outcomes in different ways. Physical and affective resources serve to reduce daily bodily pains; cognitive resources contribute more to daily task performance; and affective resources and cognitive resources are stronger predictors of self-rated creative performance.

## Job self-efficacy shapes the capacity to gain resources from physical activity

Job self-efficacy, which reflects an employee's perception of their capacity to perform their job, amplifies the resource-generating benefits of daily physical activity on sleep quality and task focus. People with higher levels of self-efficacy tend to hold stronger positive beliefs in their motivation and ability to acquire work-related resources from daily physical activity.

# How to Get More Physical

If you've found yourself moving less while working remotely, here are three research-backed ways to reap the many benefits of increasing your physical activity.

## Focus on building a habit of daily physical activity

Anything worth doing is worth doing slowly. Don't be discouraged if you don't see immediate work-related benefits from physical activity. Our research specifically examined time-lagged, next-day benefits of physical activity, demonstrating significant resource gains that contributed to performance and health payouts. Day by day, concentrate on forming new healthy habits, and results will unfold in time.

## Remember that some is better than none

We often talk ourselves out of physical activity because we're just too tired, hungry, stressed, or busy (ourselves included!). Our findings echo the perspective of the WHO, in that "some physical activity is better than doing none." To realize health benefits and minimize the harmful health effects of being sedentary, the WHO recommends that adults ages 18 to 64 years should engage in at least 2.5 hours of moderate-intensity or at least 1.25 hours of high-intensity physical activity each week.

Our research identifies moderate-intensity physical activity as most impactful for generating physical, affective, and cognitive resource gains that further benefit next-day task performance, creativity, and health outcomes. Given that low-intensity physical activity may require longer engagement to reap resource gains and high-intensity physical activity may lend itself more easily to injury, moderate-intensity exercise is a more feasible goal for many. Moreover, we found that even short periods of physical activity, even 20 minutes each day, were sufficient to generate resources that contributed to employees' next-day task performance and health.

## Motivated or not, just get moving!

Our research reveals that even employees who dislike exercising can reap benefits from daily physical activity. We also found that autonomously motivated individuals are more likely to participate in physical activity, implicating the "fun factor" as a key driver of physical activity engagement. So find an activity that makes exercise less onerous and more enjoyable. If a bootcamp session isn't your thing, try a challenging hike or a boxing class. The next time you want to swap exercise for a comfy couch, aim for just 20 minutes.

. . .

If you're looking to up your game at work, make an effort to include more physical activity in your days. Your body will thank you, and your mind will reward you with more energy, better task focus, and improved creativity.

## QUICK RECAP

If you're looking to up your game at work, try to include more physical activity in your days. Daily physical activity generates a package of next-day resources, called *resource caravans*, that contribute to work-related outcomes.

- The first resource immediately afforded by physical activity is quality sleep, or a person's degree of satisfaction with their daily sleep experience.

- The second resource acquired is vigor, an affective resource associated with energy and vitality.

- The third resource gained is task focus, a cognitive resource that supports enhanced information processing, attention, and concentration.

Adapted from content posted on hbr.org,
May 30, 2023 (product #H07O1F).

# How Taking a Vacation Improves Your Well-Being

by Rebecca Zucker

We all know that taking vacation is good for you, but it's less clear that both employers and employees understand exactly just *how good* it is for you, given that every year more than half of Americans give up paid time off. According to the U.S. Travel Association, in 2018, this amounted to 768 million days of unused vacation time, with more than 30% of it forfeited completely.[1] Add to this, the fact that over 50% of managers feel burned out.[2] Taking vacation time (and actually unplugging) has never been more important.

Perhaps you've experienced firsthand feeling recharged and refreshed from a vacation in the not-too-distant past. Or maybe you and your team have been hesitant to take a vacation because you're too busy at work.

To create more sustainability for employees (and yourself), it's important not only to regularly take available vacation time, but also to fully understand its benefits and encourage your team members to plan time off. Whether they spend their breaks lounging by a pool sipping piña coladas, doing something more active or adventurous, or even doing a staycation, going on vacation benefits their mind, body, and soul.

# Mind

The cognitive impact when you're overwhelmed with work can include cognitive fatigue, difficulty concentrating, forgetfulness, and impaired problem-solving ability, among several other effects. Taking a vacation provides greater opportunity for rest and better sleep (both quantity and quality), which can help unclutter your mind to create more mental space.

Uncluttering your mind allows you to think more clearly and boosts creativity. This can happen in both small and big ways while you're on vacation. Research shows that merely taking a walk (even if it's inside on a treadmill) significantly increases creativity.[3] On a grander scale, taking time off provides an opportunity for big or innovative ideas to emerge. Lin-Manuel Miranda conceived of *Hamilton* while on vacation. "It's no accident that the best idea I've ever had in my life—perhaps maybe the best one I'll ever have in my life—came to me on vacation," he shared. "The moment my brain got a moment's rest, *Hamilton* walked into it."[4]

Taking vacation—and even just planning for it—can also improve your mood. In particular, many people carry a significant "sleep debt" that often comes with work-related stress and anxiety. Research shows that this lack of sleep can result in negative moods such as sadness, anger, frustration, and irritability, which can, in turn, result in more difficulty sleeping.[5] Longer term, lack of sleep can also increase risk of dementia.[6] Vacation provides the opportunity to reduce or eliminate this sleep deficit. According to the American Psychological Association, getting even 60 to 90 minutes more of sleep a night can improve both memory and concentration.[7] Vacation also allows you to reset sleep patterns that can improve your mood and cognition beyond vacation. The University of Pittsburgh's Mind-Body Center found that taking vacation increases positive emotions and reduces depression.[8] And spending time in nature has been shown to reduce negative rumination and improves overall psychological well-being.

Improved rest and sleep during vacation also helps you return to work able to think more clearly as well as be more focused and productive, which has shown benefits to both the individual and the employer. An Ernst & Young study showed that for every additional 10 hours of vacation time that employees took, their year-end performance improved 8%.[9] Another study showed that using all of your vacation time increases your chances of getting a promotion or a raise.[10] Further, according to the EY study, those who took vacations more frequently were less likely to leave the firm. Similarly, in another company's experiment with taking mandatory vacation time, there were clear increases in creativity, happiness (mood), and productivity.[11] The company was also able to culturally counter any warrior or martyr mentality, where employees might otherwise be tempted to show off how hard they were working by not taking vacation time, since everyone was required to take time off at specified intervals.

# Body

Everyday work pressures can result in elevated levels of the stress hormones cortisol and epinephrine, similar to what would happen if you felt you were in physical danger. An increase in stress hormones has the effect of suppressing your immune system so your body can channel its energy to flee from (or fight) a nonexistent saber-toothed tiger. Relaxing on vacation can reduce the level of stress hormones and allow your immune system to recover, making you less prone to get sick. Conversely, if stress hormones stay chronically elevated due to the lack of rest and recovery time that results from putting off or forgoing vacation, you will not only be more susceptible to colds or the flu but also be vulnerable longer term to more serious illnesses like heart disease or cancer.

In a study of 749 women, researchers found that those who took vacation less than once every six years were eight times more likely to develop heart problems compared with those who went on vacation twice a year.[12] Going on vacation can also lower your chances of dying from coronary heart disease, help maintain lower blood sugar levels, and improve HDL or "good" cholesterol levels.

And depending on how you spend your time on vacation, there are additional potential physical benefits. Being in nature has the effect of reducing your heart rate and blood pressure. Engaging in physical activities like hiking, biking, swimming, or other water-based exercise can improve heart and respiratory health while building stronger bones and muscles and improving balance, which is more important as you age. Getting a massage is not only a great way to relax while on vacation, but has physical benefits such as improving circulation, flexibility, immune response, and decreasing muscle stiffness and joint inflammation.

## Soul

While the mental and physical benefits of vacation have been frequently touted, what is less commonly discussed is how vacation can impact us more profoundly on a deeper, more spiritual level. Our soul is our spiritual essence—it's who we really are at our core—before our families, friends, jobs, and society inundated us with messages about who we should be.

When you take time away from work to go on vacation, assuming you can mostly unplug, this break can allow you to tune out much of this external noise and tune back in to your true self. You can start to separate the striver part of you, let go of your ego, and reacquaint yourself with the essence of who you really are. When people talk about their "happy place," it's usually a place that allows them to let go of daily pressures, reconnect with themselves at a soul level, and feel a sense of peace. It's here that you are able to express your values unencumbered—whether it's adventure, learning, or beauty—and do things that bring you joy.

While it sounds hokey, answers to life's big questions—like "What do I really want?" or "What's most important to me?"—are more likely to come to us when there is some space and stillness. We get better at listening to our inner voice and can hone our intuition. Note that this quiet space can feel extremely uncomfortable for anxious overachievers, who typically have a hard time being still and not "doing." Yet it's precisely this space you have while on vacation that offers an opportunity to tap into your authentic self. This doesn't mean you need to spend your next vacation on a silent retreat at a monastery. For me, my happy place is Paris. Speaking a beautiful language, surrounding myself with art, and sitting at a café makes me feel at peace and brings me back into touch with what feels like the real me. For others, it might be sitting on a beach watching the sun set or camping in the wilderness.

When we bring our authentic selves back to work, we are more likely to shed our protective veneers, which includes not wasting energy or resources on hiding our inadequacies, so we can redirect them to the work at hand. We are also more likely to focus more on the work that has the most meaning to us, which can lead to further career-development opportunities. For some employees, this may mean leaving their current job if they realize there's a disconnect in values at their company or between who they are and what they do. And that's not necessarily a bad thing for an employer. A disengaged employee may be more expensive than one who actually quits.

. . .

The bottom line is that employees will benefit mentally, physically, and spiritually from vacation. Employers will benefit as well. And making sure your people regularly take time off is key to creating a more sustainable workplace with healthier, happier employees.

## QUICK RECAP

Making sure your employees regularly take time off is key to creating a more sustainable workplace. Research shows that taking time off benefits employees in three ways:

- **Mentally.** Taking a vacation provides greater opportunity for rest and better sleep, which can help unclutter your mind to boost creativity.

- **Physically.** Relaxing on vacation can reduce your level of stress hormones and allow your immune system to recover, making you less prone to illness.

- **Spiritually.** Answers to life's big questions—like "What do I really want?" or "What's most important to me?"—are more likely to come to us when there is some space and stillness.

Adapted from content posted on hbr.org,
July 19, 2023 (product #H07Q29).

# NOTES

## Introduction

1. Headspace Fifth Annual Workforce Attitudes Toward Mental Health Study, *A Turn of the Tide: Employee Mental Health in 2023*, May 2023, https://5327495.fs1.hubspotusercontent-na1.net/hubfs/5327495 /workforceattitudes-MAY42023.pdf.

## Chapter 1

1. Sarah Green Carmichael, "The Research Is Clear: Long Hours Backfire for People and for Companies," hbr.org, August 19, 2015.

2. Ioana Lupu, Mayra Ruiz-Castro, and Bernard Leca, "Role Distancing and the Persistence of Long Work Hours in Professional Service Firms," *Organization Studies* 43, no. 1 (2022): 7–33, https://doi.org/10.1177/0170840620934064.

3. Ann L. Cunliffe, "Reflexive Inquiry in Organizational Research: Questions and Possibilities," *Human Relations* 56, no. 8 (2003): 983–1003, https://doi.org/10.1177/00187267030568004.

## Chapter 2

1. Martina Mascali, "Hustle Culture: How 'Every Day I'm Hustlin' Became a Mantra," Monster, n.d., https://www.monster.com/career-advice/article/what -is-hustle-culture.

2. Mikaela Birgitta von Bonsdorff et al., "Working Hours and Sleep Duration in Midlife as Determinants of Health-Related Quality of Life Among Older Businessmen," *Age and Ageing* 46, no. 1 (January 2017): 108–112, https://doi.org/10.1093/ageing/afw178.

3. Derek John Clements-Croome, ed., *Creating the Productive Workplace*, 1st ed. (London: E & FN Spon, 2000).

## Chapter 3

1. Erica Pandey, "The Pandemic-Era Small Business Boom," Axios, February 15, 2022, https://www.axios.com/2022/02/15/small-business-boom -covid-recession-pandemic; Natalie Schwarz, "The Surprising Effect of the Pandemic on Graduate Degree Enrollment," *Nelnet Campus Commerce* blog,

n.d., https://campuscommerce.com/blog-effect-of-the-pandemic-on-graduate
-degree-enrollment/.

## Chapter 4

1. Robert Klara, "Sleep Deprivation Is Quietly Draining Revenue from Brands in the Covid-19 Era," *Adweek*, April 22, 2020, https://www.adweek.com /brand-marketing/sleep-deprivation-draining-revenues-covid-19/.

2. Hailey Meaklim et al., "Pre-Existing and Post-Pandemic Insomnia Symptoms Are Associated with High Levels of Stress, Anxiety, and Depression Globally During the Covid-19 Pandemic," *Journal of Clinical Sleep Medicine* 17, no. 10 (2021): 2085–2097, https://jcsm.aasm.org/doi/full/10.5664/jcsm.9354.

3. Zafir Mohd Makhbul and Zainab Rawshdeh, "Mental Stress Post-Covid-19," *International Journal of Public Health Science* 10 (2021): 194–201, https://www.researchgate.net/publication/348507556_Mental_stress_post -covid-19.

## Chapter 5

1. Emerging Technology from the arXiv archive page, "Your Brain Limits You to Just Five BFFs," *MIT Technology Review*, April 29, 2016, https://www .technologyreview.com/2016/04/29/160438/your-brain-limits-you-to-just-five-bffs/.

## Chapter 6

1. Aflac, *Workplace Benefits Trends, Employee Well-Being and Mental Health*, Aflac WorkForces Report 2022–2023, https://www.aflac.com/docs/awr/pdf/2022 -trends-and-topics/2022-aflac-awr-employee-well-being-and-mental-health.pdf.

2. Jim Harter, "U.S. Employee Engagement Needs a Rebound in 2023," Gallup, January 25, 2023, https://www.gallup.com/workplace/468233/employee -engagement-needs-rebound-2023.aspx.

3. Zhanna Lyubykh et al., "Role of Work Breaks in Well-Being and Performance: A Systematic Review and Future Research Agenda," *Journal of Occupational Health Psychology* 27, no. 5 (2022): 470–487, https://doi.org/10 .1037/ocp0000337.

4. Hongjai Rhee and Sudong Kim, "Effects of Breaks on Regaining Vitality at Work: An Empirical Comparison of 'Conventional' and 'Smart Phone' Breaks," *Computers in Human Behavior* 57 (2016): 160–167, https://www .sciencedirect.com/science/article/abs/pii/S0747563215302703.

5. Kristýna Machová, "Canine-Assisted Therapy Improves Well-Being in Nurses," in "The Psycho-Social Impact of Human-Animal Interactions," special issue, *International Journal of Environmental Research and Public Health* 16, no. 19 (2019): 3670, https://www.mdpi.com/1660-4601/16/19/3670.

6. M. Wells and R. Perrine, "Critters in the Cube Farm: Perceived Psychological and Organizational Effects of Pets in the Workplace," *Journal of Occupational Health Psychology* 6, no. 1 (2001): 81–87, https://doi.org/10.1037/1076-8998.6.1.81.

7. Tim Allen, "I'm a CEO and a Working Dad. Here's What I Wish I Did Differently," hbr.org, December 8, 2020, https://hbr.org/2020/12/im-a-ceo-and-a-working-dad-heres-what-i-wish-i-did-differently.

8. "Pandemic Pet Boom Has Increased the Demand for Pet-Friendly Workplaces," The Conversation, March 2, 2023, https://theconversation.com/pandemic-pet-boom-has-increased-the-demand-for-pet-friendly-workplaces-200217.

## Chapter 7

1. "Research," Impact Players website, The Wiseman Group, n.d., https://impactplayersbook.com/wp-content/uploads/2021/10/impact-players-research-process.pdf.

2. "Workplace Stress," American Institute of Stress, https://www.stress.org/workplace-stress.

3. CPP Global Human Capital Report, *Workplace Conflict and How Businesses Can Harness It to Thrive*, CPP, July 2008, https://img.en25.com/Web/CPP/Conflict_report.pdf.

4. The Wiseman Group, "The Rookie Smarts Research," https://thewisemangroup.com/books/rookie-smarts/research/.

## Chapter 8

1. "The Anatomy of Work Global Index," https://asana.com/resources/anatomy-of-work.

2. World Health Organization, "Burn-Out an 'Occupational Phenomenon': International Classification of Diseases," WHO Departmental News, May 28, 2019, https://www.who.int/news/item/28-05-2019-burn-out-an-occupational-phenomenon-international-classification-of-diseases.

## Chapter 9

1. Gallup, *State of the Global Workplace: 2023 Report*, Gallup, https://www.gallup.com/workplace/349484/state-of-the-global-workplace-2022-report.aspx#ite-393248.

2. "Stress and the Role of Perception," Stress Management for Health Course, n.d., https://stresscourse.tripod.com/id100.html.

3. Benjamin Kaveladze and Alan R. Teo, "New Study Explores How Social Relationships Protect Against the Harmful Effects of Stress," *On the Brain* blog,

January 26, 2021, https://blogs.ohsu.edu/brain/2021/01/26/new-study-explores
-how-social-relationships-protect-against-the-harmful-effects-of-stress/.

## Chapter 10

1. Jesús Montero-Marín and Javier García-Campayo, "A Newer and
Broader Definition of Burnout: Validation of the 'Burnout Clinical Subtype
Questionnaire (BCSQ-36)," *BMC Public Health* 10, no. 302 (2010), https://doi
.org/10.1186/1471-2458-10-302.

2. Montero-Marín and García-Campayo, "A Newer and Broader Definition
of Burnout."

## Chapter 12

1. Rebecca Alexander et al., "The Neuroscience of Positive Emotions and
Affect: Implications for Cultivating Happiness and Wellbeing," *Neuroscience &
Biobehavioral Reviews* 121 (2021): 220–249, https://doi.org/10.1016/j.neubiorev
.2020.12.002.

2. Amantha Imber, "Dan Heath on Curing Himself from Procrastination,
Solving Problems Before They Happen, and the Ideal Time to Seek Feedback,"
March 4, 2020, in *How I Work*, podcast, 54 min., https://www.amantha.com
/podcasts/dan-health-on-curing-himself-from-procrastination-solving-problems
-before-they-happen-and-the-ideal-time-to-seek-feedback/.

## Chapter 14

1. Linda Babcock, Maria P. Recalde, Lise Vesterlund, and Laurie Weingart,
"Gender Differences in Accepting and Receiving Requests for Tasks with Low
Promotability," *American Economic Review* 107, no. 3 (March 2017): 714–747,
https://pubs.aeaweb.org/doi/pdfplus/10.1257/aer.20141734.

2. Babcock et al., "Gender Differences in Accepting and Receiving Requests."

## Chapter 15

1. Branka Vuleta, "Generation Z Statistics," *99 Firms* blog, n.d., https://
99firms.com/blog/generation-z-statistics/#gref.

2. Amantha Imber, "Ultralearner Scott Young on How to Dramatically
Improve the Way You Learn," November 27, 2019, in *How I Work*, podcast,
51 min., https://www.amantha.com/podcasts/ultralearner-scott-young-on-how
-to-dramatically-improve-the-way-you-learn/.

3. dscout, *Mobile Touches: dscout's Inaugural Study of Humans and Their
Tech*, dscout, June 15, 2016, https://pages.dscout.com/hubfs/downloads/dscout
_mobile_touches_study_2016.pdf?_ga=2.180416224.67221035.1650551540
-199217915.1650551540.

## Chapter 16

1. Columbia University Mailman School of Public Health, "Covid-19 Pandemic Impacts Mental Health Worldwide," News, March 18, 2021, https://www.publichealth.columbia.edu/public-health-now/news/covid-19 -pandemic-impacts-mental-health-worldwide.

2. Deloitte Global Talent, "Millennials, Gen Z and Mental Health, Managing Mental Health in the Workplace," Deloitte, June 2020, https://www .deloitte.com/content/dam/assets-shared/legacy/docs/about/2022/gx-millennial -survey-mental-health-whitepaper.pdf.

3. Ipsos, "Mental Health in the Workplace: Global Impact Study," Ipsos News and Events, October 9, 2019, https://www.ipsos.com/en/mental-health -workplace-global-impact-study.

4. Anup Jayaram, "92% of Indian Employees Prefer Discussing Mental Health Issues with Robots Than Managers," *Business Today*, October 11, 2020, https://www.businesstoday.in/latest/corporate/story/92-percent-of-indian -employees-prefer-discussing-mental-health-issues-with-robots-than-managers -275394-2020-10-11.

5. Massachusetts Department of Mental Health, "Why Is It Important to Talk About Mental Health?" Massachusetts Office of Health and Human Services, n.d., https://www.mass.gov/info-details/why-is-it-important-to-talk -about-mental-health.

## Chapter 17

1. Michael T. Ford, Christopher P. Cerasoli, Jennifer A. Higgins, and Andrew L. Decesare, "Relationships Between Psychological, Physical, and Behavioural Health and Work Performance: A Review and Meta-Analysis," *Work & Stress* 25, no. 33 (2011): 185–204, DOI: 10.1080/02678373.2011. 609035.

2. Stewart D. Friedman and Alyssa Westring, "Empowering Individuals to Integrate Work and Life: Insights for Management Development," *Journal of Management Development* 34, no. 3 (April 13, 2015), https://www.emerald.com /insight/content/doi/10.1108/JMD-11-2012-0144/full/html.

## Chapter 19

1. World Health Organization, "Physical Activity," WHO Fact Sheet, n.d., https://www.who.int/news-room/fact-sheets/detail/physical-activity.

2. Yolanda Na Li, Bonnie Hayden Cheng, Bingjie Yu, and Julie N. Y. Zhu, "Let's Get Physical! A Time-Lagged Examination of the Motivation for Daily Physical Activity and Implications for Next-Day Performance and Health," *Personnel Psychology* (March 17, 2023), https://doi.org/10.1111/peps .12585.

## Chapter 20

1. "Time Off and Vacation Usage," US Travel Association, https://www
.ustravel.org/toolkit/time-and-vacation-usage.

2. Dawn Klinghoffer and Katie Kirkpatrick-Husk, "More Than 50% of
Managers Feel Burned Out," hbr.org, May 18, 2023, https://hbr.org/2023/05
/more-than-50-of-managers-feel-burned-out.

3. May Wong, "Stanford Study Finds Walking Improves Creativity," News,
Stanford University web site, April 24, 2014, https://news.stanford.edu/2014/04
/24/walking-vs-sitting-042414/.

4. Anna Almendrala, "Lin-Manuel Miranda: It's 'No Accident' Hamilton
Came to Me on Vacation," *HuffPost*, June 23, 2016, https://www.huffpost.com
/entry/lin-manuel-miranda-says-its-no-accident-hamilton-inspiration-struck-on
-vacation_n_576c136ee4b0b489bb0ca7c2.

5. Department of Health, "Mood and Sleep," State Government of Victoria,
Australia, website, https://www.betterhealth.vic.gov.au/health/healthyliving
/Mood-and-sleep#sleep-and-moods.

6. Erin Bryant, National Institutes of Health, "Lack of Sleep in Middle Age
May Increase Dementia Risk," NIH Research Matters, April 27, 2021,
https://www.nih.gov/news-events/nih-research-matters/lack-sleep-middle-age
-may-increase-dementia-risk.

7. "More Sleep Would Make Us Happier, Healthier and Safer," American
Psychological Association, 2014, https://www.apa.org/topics/sleep/deprivation
-consequences.

8. "Road Trip! Health Net Points Out the Health Benefits of Vacations,"
Healthnet, https://www.healthnet.com/portal/home/content/iwc/home/articles
/health_benefits_of_vacations.action.

9. "Road Trip! Health Net Points Out the Health Benefits of Vacations,"
Health Net, n.d., https://www.healthnet.com/portal/home/content/iwc/home
/articles/health_benefits_of_vacations.action.

10. Shawn Achor, "Are the People Who Take Vacations the Ones Who Get
Promoted?," hbr.org, June 12, 2015, https://hbr.org/2015/06/are-the-people-who
-take-vacations-the-ones-who-get-promoted.

11. Neil Pasricha and Shashank Nigam, "What One Company Learned from
Forcing Employees to Use Their Vacation Time," hbr.org, August 11, 2017,
https://hbr.org/2017/08/what-one-company-learned-from-forcing-employees-to
-use-their-vacation-time.

12. Hilary Brueck, "What Taking a Vacation Does to Your Body and Brain,"
*Insider*, September 1, 2018, https://www.businessinsider.com/vacation-health
-benefits-2018-8#researchers-who-followed-a-group-of-749-women-from
-massachusetts-for-two-decades-found-that-those-who-went-on-vacation-less
-than-once-every-six-years-were-nearly-eight-times-more-likely-to-develop-heart
-problems-than-women-who-vacationed-twice-a-year-9.

# INDEX

# ABOUT THE CONTRIBUTORS

**MORRA AARONS-MELE** is the author of *The Anxious Achiever: Turn Your Biggest Fears into Your Leadership Superpower* (Harvard Business Review Press, 2023). She has written for the *New York Times*, *Wall Street Journal*, *O* magazine, and other publications, and is the host of the *Anxious Achiever* podcast from LinkedIn Presents.

**LINDA BABCOCK** is a professor of economics at Carnegie Mellon University. She is the author of *Women Don't Ask* and *Ask for It*. A behavioral economist, she is the founder and director of PROGRESS, which pursues positive social change for women and girls through education, partnerships, and research.

**BONNIE HAYDEN CHENG** is an associate professor of management and the MBA program director at HKU Business School, University of Hong Kong. She is the chief resilience officer of Human at Work, serves as a scientific adviser of OneMind at Work, and is a subject-matter expert for the Academy of Management. She works with senior executives of companies ranging from startups to *Fortune* 500, transforming corporate cultures by incorporating wellness into their business strategy.

**IAN DALEY** is a leadership development expert with over 15 years of progressive management experience in the health care sector, with companies such as Novartis, Novo Nordisk, and

GlaxoSmithKline. He is the founder of Daley & Co, a leadership consulting and training firm, and is the creator of the *New Leader* podcast, focused on developing new managers and aspiring leaders. You can follow him on LinkedIn, where he shares his insight and expertise with over 24,000 followers.

**RUSSELL GLASS** is the CEO of Headspace, leading the company's mission to transform mental health care to improve the health and happiness of the world. As a serial entrepreneur, Russ has held multiple CEO roles, most recently at Ginger, prior to its merger with Headspace in 2021, which resulted in the creation of an end-to-end mental health platform. He formerly led products for the marketing solutions group at LinkedIn and is the founder and former CEO and president of Bizo, a B2B marketing and data platform, which he sold to LinkedIn in 2014. While at Bizo, Russ coauthored *The Big Data-Driven Business*, a guide for how companies can use big data to drive better decision-making and results. He is also the author of the children's book *Voting with a Porpoise*, and serves on the board of the nonprofit Rock the Vote, where he leverages his expertise in technology, data science, and branding to increase engagement and turnout among young voters. Russ has a BSE degree in mechanical engineering and economics from Duke University.

**DUYGU BIRICIK GULSEREN** is an assistant professor at the School of Human Resources Management at York University, Toronto, Canada, and chair of the Canadian Society for Industrial and Organizational Psychology. Her research focuses on healthy work and leadership.

**AMANTHA IMBER** is an organizational psychologist, the author of the international bestseller *Time Wise*, the founder of behavior change consultancy Inventium, and the host of *How I Work*, a podcast about the habits and rituals of the world's most successful people.

**BRENDAN P. KEEGAN** serves as chairman, CEO, and president at Merchants Fleet and was recently named the World's Most Innovative CEO by CEO World Awards. Keegan is also the silver winner of Executive of the Year by Best in Biz Awards and a Stevie Awards bronze winner by American Business Awards.

**JANNA KORETZ** is a psychologist and the founder of Azimuth, which provides therapy focused on the unique challenges of individuals in high-pressure careers.

**YOLANDA NA LI** is an assistant professor in the department of management, Lingnan University, Hong Kong. Her research focuses on understanding how various nonwork activities affect work outcomes, why individuals may perform different unethical behaviors at work and their consequences, and the role of emotions in the workplace.

**IOANA LUPU** is an associate professor at ESSEC Business School France. She is interested in overwork, mental health, and performance measurement in knowledge-intensive settings such as audit, consulting, and law firms. Follow her on LinkedIn and visit www.ioanalupu.com.

**ZHANNA LYUBYKH** is an assistant professor of management and organization studies at the Beedie School of Business, Simon Fraser University, Vancouver, Canada. Her research focuses on employee well-being, workplace mistreatment, and leadership.

**DONNA MCGEORGE** is a bestselling author and global authority on productivity. Her book series, It's About Time, covers meetings, structuring your day, and doing more with less.

**BRENDA PEYSER** has held leadership positions in the corporate world and academia for over 30 years. Most recently, she was a professor of communications at Carnegie Mellon, where she also served as associate dean of the School of Public Policy and Management and was the founding executive director of Carnegie Mellon University Australia.

**MAYRA RUIZ-CASTRO** is a senior lecturer (associate professor) at Queen Mary University of London, United Kingdom. Her research focuses on equality in organizations and households. Find and follow her on LinkedIn.

**JOE SANOK** is the host of the popular *The Practice of the Practice* podcast, which is recognized as one of the Top 50 podcasts worldwide with over 100,000 downloads each month. Bestselling authors, experts and scholars, and business leaders and innovators are featured and interviewed in the 900-plus podcasts he has done over the last 10 years. Joe is also the author of *Thursday Is the New Friday*, a book for businesses that want to implement the four-day workweek.

**ELIZABETH GRACE SAUNDERS** is a time management coach and the founder of Real Life E Time Coaching & Speaking. She is the author of *How to Invest Your Time like Money* and *Divine Time Management*.

**VASUNDHARA SAWHNEY** is a senior editor at *Harvard Business Review*.

**CARSON TATE** is the founder and managing partner of Working Simply, a business consulting firm that partners with organizations, business leaders, and employees to enhance workplace productivity, foster employee engagement, and build personal and professional legacies. She is the author of *Own It. Love It. Make It Work: How to Make Any Job Your Dream Job*.

**LISE VESTERLUND** is a professor of economics at the University of Pittsburgh and directs the Pittsburgh Experimental Economics Laboratory and the Behavioral Economic Design Initiative. Published in leading economic journals, her research has been covered by NPR, the *New York Times*, the *Washington Post*, ABC, *The Economist*, *The Atlantic*, *The Guardian*, *Chicago Tribune*, and *Forbes*.

**LAURIE R. WEINGART** is a management professor at Carnegie Mellon University. She has served as CMU's interim provost and chief academic officer and as a senior associate dean and director of the Accelerate Leadership Center. Her award-winning research has been covered by the *New York Times* and *Business Insider* and published in top management and psychology journals.

**ALYSSA F. WESTRING** is the Vincent de Paul Professor and Chair of the Department of Management and Entrepreneurship at DePaul University's Driehaus College of Business. She is the coauthor of *Parents Who Lead: The Leadership Approach You Need to Parent with Purpose, Fuel Your Career, and Create a Richer Life.*

**MELODY WILDING** is an executive coach and the author of *Trust Yourself: Stop Overthinking and Channel Your Emotions for Success at Work.*

**LIZ WISEMAN** is the author of *Impact Players*, *Rookie Smarts*, and *Multipliers* and CEO of the Wiseman Group. You can connect with her on X/Twitter @LizWiseman.

**REBECCA ZUCKER** is an executive coach and a founding partner at Next Step Partners, a leadership development firm. Her clients have included Amazon, Clorox, Morrison Foerster, Norwest Venture Partners, the James Irvine Foundation, and high-growth technology companies like DocuSign and Dropbox. You can follow her on X/Twitter @rszucker.

# Accelerate your career with HBR's Work Smart Series.

If you enjoyed this book and want more career advice from *Harvard Business Review*, turn to other books in **HBR's Work Smart Series**. Each title explores the topics that matter most to you as you start out in your career: being yourself at work, collaborating with (sometimes difficult) colleagues, maintaining your mental health, and more. **HBR's Work Smart Series** books are your go-to guides to step into and move forward successfully in your professional world.

**store.hbr.org**

Buy for your team, clients, or event.
Visit hbr.org/bulksales for quantity discount rates.

 **Harvard Business Review**